Stepping
OUT OF THE
Shadows

Stepping
OUT OF THE
Shadows

[Re]Connecting with Your Life's Journey

Dr. Steve Frisch, Psy.D.

ALIVE & WELL PUBLICATIONS
CHICAGO, ILLINOIS

Although the author and publisher have made every effort to ensure the accuracy and completeness of information contained in this book, we assume no responsibility for errors, inaccuracies, omissions, or any inconsistency herein. Any slights of people, places, or organizations are unintentional.

Book cover and text design by Mary J. Burroughs.

Publisher's Cataloging in Publication

Frisch, Steve.
    Stepping out of the shadows : (re)connecting with your life's journey / Steve Frisch.
    p. cm.
    Preassigned LCCN: 97-93780
    ISBN 0-9651511-3-1

    1. Self-actualization (Psychology).   I. Title.
BF637.S4F75 1998   158
                                 QBI97-40672

For years I have been the collector of a wide variety of quotations. Too often, however I carelessly neglected to note sources. In preparing this book I have spent countless hours attempting, unsuccessfully to locate the origins of some of the quotations cited. If you know the sources, please contact me at the numbers listed in this book. My apologies to the authors, and to the readers for the absence of credit.

ATTENTION ORGANIZATIONS, CORPORATIONS, HEALING CENTERS, AND SCHOOLS OF SPIRITUAL DEVELOPMENT:

Quantity discounts are available on bulk purchases of this book for educational purposes, fund raising, or gift giving. Special books, booklets, or book excerpts can be created to fit specific needs for promotion of your organizational missions. For information, please contact Alive And Well Publications, 1330 N. Dearborn Suite 1205, Chicago, IL 60610 or call (773) 477-8959.

Table of Contents

Acknowledgments

The wisdom contained within the pages of this book has been woven from the shared experiences it has been my privilege to enjoy with so very many special people. Although you are too numerous to mention, I trust that you all appreciate how much you have meant to me. Thank you all for including me in your lives.

The creation of this book was a collaborative effort with many truly gifted people. I especially want to express my gratitude to my editor and publication designer.

To Donna. You worked hard rounding the manuscript into readable condition. I greatly appreciate your hard work. All that is right about this book is due to your talents, any uncorrected mistakes are reflective only of my stubbornness. Thank you!

To Mary Burroughs, our publication designer and creative director, you continue to outdo yourself. Thanks for keeping the dream alive!

With any work I complete, I always take pause to acknowledge the gratitude I feel towards my teachers. You have come in all shapes and sizes, but it is your essence that resonates within the pages of this book. Thank you all so very, very much!

Dedication

In loving memory of my best friend, Karen.
In a life that has been blessed with much abundance,
you were the most precious gift ever sent to me.
Your incredible spirit brightened my world in a
way that I had never experienced before. Please know
that your spirit will always live in my heart.
You have my everlasting love and gratitude for having
invited me into your world.

About the Author

Dr. Frisch is a clinical psychologist in private practice in Chicago, Illinois. He is a graduate of the Adler School of Professional Psychology where he received his doctorate in clinical psychology. He received his Masters Degree from the National College of Education where he specialized in addictions counseling. His undergraduate degree was awarded to him by the University of Cincinnati, where he graduated with honors.

Dr. Frisch received post-doctoral training in two specialties at the Adler School of Professional Psychology. He completed a certificate training program in clinical hypnosis at the Center For The Advanced Study Of Clinical Hypnosis. He also completed a certificate training program in marriage and family counseling. He is licensed by the state of Illinois as a clinical psychologist. He is certified in Illinois by IAODAPCA as a certified drug and alcohol counselor.

Dr. Frisch's first book, *The Comparative Effectiveness of Group Therapy Versus Individual Therapy As Measured By Self-Concept, Interpersonal Orientation, and Degree of Emotional Adjustment* was an empirical investigation of the treatment modalities he utilizes in his private practice. This book was based on a study he conducted to demonstrate the effectiveness of his treatment protocols.

He has since written the *Bridge-Builders* series, which focuses on the development and enrichment of relationships. As well, he has written the *Pathfinders* series, which focuses on personal growth and self-actualization.

His treatment philosophy has grown out of his diverse clinical background in which he has worked with a variety of different clinical populations. From these diverse experiences, Dr. Frisch has assimilated a variety of assessment and treatment interventions into his integrated treatment philosophy.

Dr. Frisch has worked on the staff of both inpatient and outpatient chemical dependency programs. This experience provided the foundation for his work with issues that arise from the impact of chemical dependency on the individual, the family, and the workplace.

As a result of his work in the field of chemical dependency, Dr. Frisch founded the Adult Children Institute. This treatment clinic specialized in working with adults who were raised in families that were emotionally organized around the influences of drugs and alcohol, sexual and physical abuse, and emotional neglect.

The Adult Children Institute developed treatment interventions that enabled the program's participants to develop effective ways to heal from the aftereffects of trauma they experienced from their earlier development. These aftereffects included substance abuse, depression, anxiety, low self-esteem, shame, and relationship issues such as fear of emotional intimacy and commitment.

Dr. Frisch co-developed and was the coordinator of a mental health program for homeless adults who required treatment for substance abuse and emotional disorders. He developed an individualized assessment and treatment protocol that provided the impetus and support for each individual to rebuild their lives within their local communities.

The Relationship Bridge Building and Pathfinders personal growth programs represent the integration of Dr. Frisch's ongoing research and work in the area of human growth and potential development. Program participants develop the necessary awareness and skills to create an empowered life that maximizes their full potential for both their interpersonal and professional lives.

Whether by individual consultation, group experiences, workshops, or seminars, Dr. Frisch engages his audiences with a mixture of common sense and sound psychological principles of change to awaken and inspire their dormant potential. He consults with individuals, couples, groups, and organizations that are seeking to implement the principles of development, change, and growth in their lives.

About the
Stepping Out of the Shadows Program

When asked how he was able to create his artistic wonders from mere pieces of marble, Michelangelo is said to have replied, "I didn't do anything. God put them in the marble, they were already there. I had only to carve away the parts that kept you from seeing them."

Much like Michelangelo's marvelous statues, our lives are ever unfolding miracles of transformation. Transforming our lives from a never ending cycle of despair, fear, and fragmentation to one of hopefulness, wellness, and wholeness is the purpose of the *Stepping Out of the Shadows* program.

All that the human experience is about is our journey toward wholeness—a wholeness forged from the aspects of ourselves that we are aware of with the aspects of ourselves that we have disowned, existing only within the *shadows* of our awareness.

So much of who we are we have disowned. Many of us have been taught not to express certain parts of who we are. However these parts, like jealousy, lust, greed, anger, and selfishness take on a life of their own when hidden in the shadows.

These disowned aspects of who we are do not live quietly in the shadows. These parts seek to be expressed, to be seen in the light of day as integrated parts of who we are. At the same time, we expend an enormous amount of energy pushing these parts away from our awareness. The energy we expend contributes to much of the despair and emotional discomfort we experience in our lives. The essential drama that leaves us feeling so fragmented is the underlying ongoing psychological and spiritual conflict between the parts of ourselves that we know and the parts that are demanding to be known.

In order to become whole, we need to reclaim all of these disowned aspects. Think for a moment about all the things that you deny about yourself. Vulnerability? Emotional expressiveness? How comfortable are you expressing your softness, compassion, and playfulness? Creativity may live within you but never be expressed. How safe do you feel expressing your anger, your sexuality, all the good, the bad and the ugly about who you are? Yet it is these very qualities—not given expression, forever pushed further and further away—that take up space in the shadows of your life, oftentimes creating chaos, and ultimately leaving you disconnected from your life's journey.

Reclaiming those parts of ourselves forever unrealized, unacknowledged, and disowned, requires us to look deeply within. For stepping out of the shadows is a process of self-examination, of making the unconscious conscious. By honestly looking inside and discovering these *old-new* pieces of who we are, we can begin to view ourselves in new ways. Quite simply, the process of stepping out of the shadows is the path that enables us to emancipate the rest of our humanity, wisdom, and compassion, thereby healing the relationship we have with ourselves, enriching the relationships we have with the people in our lives, and creating an understanding of the meaning of our life and our connection to a higher power within our universe.

Stepping out of the shadows affords us the opportunity to bring greater balance to our lives. Challenged to heal the relationship we have with ourselves, we may finally create a space of self-acceptance rather than self-condemnation. Challenged to affect essential shifts with the people in our lives, we can transform our relationships from one of isolated independence or enmeshed dependence to one of supportive interdependence. This newly created space of interdependence will lift our relationships out of the quagmire of fear, control, retribution, and judgment. When this shift takes place within us, as the totality of who we are finally emerges, we will begin to accept the full humanity of ourselves and the people in our lives with all of its blotches and blemishes.

Taking ownership of all of who we are and emerging whole, we will feel safer and freer in our day to day lives. Unburdening ourselves with the need to keep our guard up, we will no longer live in fear of being found out for who we fear ourselves to be. A new found openness towards others will accompany our new found self-acceptance. Developing a deeper, kinder knowledge of our inner selves will free us to be more available to the people in our lives: free to create authentic intimacy with the people who matter most. This new found level of intimacy will create a new sense of safety as we feel more grounded in our world.

Reclaiming those parts of ourselves abandoned to the shadows of our awareness will enable a healing process to unfold within us. A sense of wholeness will emerge where once there was only the pain from our many fragmented wounded selves.

No longer will we expend the enormous amount of emotional energy it takes to keep aspects of who we are hidden from ourselves and the world. Life will begin to feel lighter, easier. We will begin to learn through our new found wisdom the choices that enable us to release patterns of negativity, doubt, and fear, that are no longer appropriate to who we are and what we are becoming.

Authentic empowerment can only be gained by making choices that stretch us in ways that take us from the incomplete beings we are to more fully integrated, whole souls. When we finally step out of the shadows, we will create a new place for ourselves in the universe. No longer will we empower ourselves through the familiar tactics of control and intimidation. We will be able to respond to the events in our lives rather than merely react. Finally, we will be able to discard the tools of avoidance and withdrawing as we discover the joy of living a life of empowerment rather than enduring a life of paralysis.

*If he [the teacher] is indeed wise, he does not
bid you enter the house of his wisdom, but rather
leads you to the threshold of your own.*

-Kahil Gibran

Let's Start at the Very Beginning...

Our most profound existential urge is to grow and evolve. We all are moved by our inner quest to find meaning, to create a sense of orientation in the universe. I can't think of anybody who isn't hungering for a deeper sense of purpose in their lives, a deeper connection to the underlying forces of life.

The path we follow to quench our thirst for meaning and growth is a process of transformation fraught with challenging milestones along the way. Each step of the process presents us with different obstacles from which valuable lessons can be learned about ourselves. These lessons are the source from which enlightenment sheds its brilliance on our path, enabling us to find our way out of the darkness of the shadows and discovering the means by which we can [re]connect to our life's journey.

I have written this book to assist you in your own searching. Included in *Stepping Out of the Shadows* are the lessons I have discovered in my own searching, as well those I have learned from guiding others on their own personal journey.

But more than just a guide for your journey, this book is a special invitation. An invitation to shrink your ego and expand your soul. An invitation to explore and discover. To create a personal blueprint for your emotional and spiritual well-being. A blueprint that will reveal to you the path to a life of emotional richness and well-being.

Come explore within yourself. Explore the festering

wounds that hold you back, that tend to appear in your life in ways that limit you. Wounds that never seemingly heal. Wounds that leave you feeling estranged from yourself, the people in your life, and the purpose your life serves.

Throughout the years, it has been my privilege to share this journey with people just like you. We've touched the depth of despair as well as ascended unimaginable heights. Through my own journey, as well as my work with others, I have learned much. One thing I have discovered is that in order to step out of the shadows so that we may [re]connect with our life's journey, we all will inevitably encounter a series of passageways as we follow our evolutionary path of growth and becoming.

This book is my attempt at presenting to you what process we follow as we step out of the shadows. Because the telling of a story is only two dimensional while our lives are three-dimensional, it's impossible to capture the true interrelated nature of these passageways. Although I present each passageway of the process in a particular order, you will encounter them in your life in a continually evolving, ever-changing interdependent fashion.

I've divided this book into eight sections. The first section will provide you with an overview of the journey that lies ahead. Following the first section, I present to you each of the seven passageways we will walk through together on this very special journey.

Each section of the book is intended to serve as a mirror for you to look into—an opportunity to find yourself in each stage of transformation. For many of you, a specific section may serve as a rearview mirror. You may discover that you have already *walked the walk* of a certain section. Use such a section as a way of measuring how far you have already come, as well as reflect upon what the lessons of that process were for you. For others, each section will serve as a beacon of light, shedding a bright ray of hope where now there is only darkness.

I have included in each section what I call *Pathfinder's Tips*. These tips will enable you to either begin or to continue your very personal work. Beyond providing you with specific tools to enhance your journey, there are exercises throughout the book that will enable you to more personally explore the material covered.

What follows is a short overview of the sections contained in the book.

Awakening the Soul focuses on the toxic influences that deaden the soul as well as the means to awaken what we have buried so deep within ourselves that we have lost touch with those parts of ourselves.

Liberating the Spirit explores how we bind our spirit in such a fashion that our lives become emotionally and spiritually dead. In this section, we examine what our spirit is and how we can set our spirit free.

Illuminating the Path provides a direction for us to focus our efforts on. Once our soul has awakened and our spirit has been liberated, this section will provide a means for self-examination in order that we can create the necessary focus for our journey.

Transforming the Mindset is an important section for anyone who is seeking to unlock the prison that their mind creates for themselves. We explore how to free ourselves from the prison of inflexible thinking as well as create the joy we might experience from living a life grounded in the here-and-now.

Healing Your Wounds paints a picture of ways we can change the relationship we have with ourselves. The very quality of this relationship we have with ourselves is very much connected to the depth of well-being we experience in our lives.

Strengthening the Bonds of Fellowship focuses on our need to connect to the people who matter most to us in a very special way. We will discover how our relationships are the most important antidote for a spirit that has been ravaged by loneliness and alienation.

Rhythm of Life enables us to put into perspective what our journey can be like, as well as some specific pointers that we all need to bear in mind as we stay involved with our personal growth.

The journey you and I are about to embark upon is unique—unique because no two people will experience the material in this book the same way. No two people will find the same material equally important or irrelevant.

Just one word of caution as you begin. There's nothing here that needs to be *learned*. But there's much here for you to *experience* so that you may *learn*. Do the best you can to *patiently* work with the material that is presented to you. My only intention in writing this book is to light a thousand small fires to illuminate your path as you step out of the shadows and [re]connect to your life's journey.

PART 1

Stepping Out of the Shadows

I prepared excitedly for my departure, as if this journey had a mysterious significance. I had decided to change my mode of life. "Till now," I told myself, "you have only seen the shadow and been well content with it; now, I am going to lead you to the substance.

-Nikos Kazantzakis,
from *Zorba the Greek*

The First Step
of the Longest March

Do not look back in anger, or forward in fear,
but around in awareness.

-James Thurber

We had been working together long enough for me to know exactly how she would react to what I had to say to her. That's what was so intriguing about the therapist-client relationship we had developed. No matter what pearls of wisdom I tried to offer her, she would always just roll her eyes as she looked at me and say, "Whatever!"

Well, she was having a particularly difficult week in what had been a particularly difficult six months. Through all the ups and downs that we had gone through together, I don't think that I had ever seen her quite as agitated as she was on this particular day.

Her face had turned crimson red from the anger and futility consuming her. She couldn't spit her words out fast enough, seemingly trying to exorcise the pain that had enveloped her life.

She was feeling like her life had hit a dead end from which she would never recover as she looked at me and howled, "When is this all going to end for me?!"

I considered her question carefully, knowing full well what the answer was, knowing all too well what her response to my answer would be.

I was carefully measuring what my response should be when I decided to just go for broke and lay on her what I considered to be the solution that each and everyone of us must discover for ourselves.

So, I steeled myself for her reaction as I said, "All of this will change when you make certain shifts in the relationship you have with yourself, the relationship you have with the people in your life, and the relationship you have with your spiritual power."

I held my breath waiting for the inevitable rolling of her eyes, the utterance of her dismissive, "Whatever!"

She thought about what I had to say for a moment, all the while looking at me as if I were crazy. Finally she snarled at me, "Oh, that's just great! That should only take me about forty years!"

I looked right back at her and responded, "You may be right. When are you going to get started?"

With that said, her face kind of softened as the faintest of smiles began to form in each corner of her mouth. She thought about my challenge for a moment, finally saying, "All right, Steve, let's rock and roll. My way sure as hell ain't working, let's give something else a shot."

As a clinical psychologist, I work with people everyday who are searching for the means to create those very shifts in their lives, shifts in their relationships with themselves and the people who matter most, shifts that enable them to step out of the shadows and [re]connect with their life's journey.

You may recognize the feelings we experience when we become disconnected from our path. Confusion, chronic anger, hopelessness, emptiness, despair, boredom, alienation from ourselves and others. But no matter how we ultimately go about the search, we all are searching for one thing and one thing only—the path that will lead us out of the shadows, the path by which we can become whole and integrated.

The aim of that search is simply to reveal to ourselves two things: the essence of who we are and what path to follow in order to express that essence in our day-to-day life. This search arises out of the different choices we make as we chart a direction, a direction that fills our lives with either purpose or emptiness.

We all recognize the emptiness that paralyzes us as we make those choices that disconnect us from the path of our life's journey. You recognize the ways your being lost and disconnected appears in your life, don't you?

We may feel stuck in our professional lives. Perhaps our jobs have become merely a means to an end. An end that provides us with economic survival, but not an end that honors the essence of what our abilities and interests are.

We may feel no sense of involvement, no sense of being connected to our community. Perhaps we feel isolated and alienated from the world in which we live.

We may feel stuck in our relationships with our family and friends. Perhaps we become lost in our relationships, overwhelmed by what our relationships take from us but don't return in kind.

Or it may be that we've never become grounded with a long-lasting relationship with our spiritual power. A relationship that provides us with guidance and direction for the purpose from which we live our lives.

Finally, it may be that we've become estranged from ourselves. Perhaps the relationship we have with ourselves limits our ability to live in the world in a way that nurtures our growth and leaves us feeling safe with other people.

Whatever the reasons for being disconnected from our life's journey, we all have within ourselves the means to discover the path that will lead us out of the darkness to a place of light.

You see, we all hold the answers within ourselves to the questions that we confront on a daily basis. We possess the wisdom to guide ourselves, in however an imperfect way we create, to the destiny we all are seeking to connect with. Each and everyone of us possess the courage necessary to heal our wounds and grow from the pain that any process of healing involves.

Make no mistake about this. The path that leads us out of the shadows is a richly rewarding experience.

Creating a life that is rich with the love and support of those who matter the most to us is a reward like no other you can imagine.

Creating a life that is an expression of who you genuinely are is the most uplifting gift you can give to yourself.

Creating a life that is closely connected to a spiritual power provides a sense of stability and strength that will guide you through the roughest storms you can imagine.

Creating a life that is built upon the bedrock of a loving nurturing relationship with yourself will enable you to attract the kind of people in your life that will mirror your own self-acceptance rather than tear you down.

No matter how much training we've received to believe differently, I know that it can happen for us all. Yet, we will all experience much pain and discomfort as we wrestle with letting go of our old ways. We will experience much fear as we search for new ways of acting and thinking that will keep us connected to our new path.

Yet, the outcome of our struggle and triumphs, the outcome of our pain and healing, the outcome of our letting go will be our emergence from the shadows as we begin to [re]connect with our life's journey. A journey that will fill our lives with abundance, the abundance of self-love, receiving love and caring from others, and the freedom to express ourselves in ways that honor who we are.

The Heart of the Matter

With all the miseries surrounding us, threatening our destruction, we still have an instinct that we cannot repress, which elevates us above our sorrows.

-Pascal

We were finishing up our last session. This was a time for reflection. Looking back upon where we started, understanding where we were today.

"I can see so much more clearly today how lost I was back then. I remember thinking then that I wasn't the one with the problem, everyone else had a problem."

As my client was speaking, I was reminiscing in my own mind about our first session together, what brought him to my office, what it was that he said he needed to work out. I especially remembered how angry he had become with me in that first session, so I casually brought that up to him.

"That's right, I remember now. My fiancée had given me a pamphlet you had written, I don't remember what it was about."

"Seven Steps to Emotional and Spiritual Well-Being," I reminded him.

"Oh yea, something like that. But I do remember telling you that I understood what you had explained in the pamphlet, I just didn't understand how to go about doing it.

"So I thought I would ask you to explain, little did I know then what I know only too well about you now, you refused to explain."

"I refused to explain?" I responded, not quite remembering things the way he had remembered them.

"Well, you gave me what I thought was a bunch of double-talk. Something like, 'Those steps are not something that can be *taught* to you, they are something for you to *discover*. Ultimately, you must discover your own solutions to the challenges in your life, rather than live out somebody else's solutions.'"

I laughed at his sarcasm as he tried to mimic me. "Well, we got through that first obstacle. Do you remember what those seven steps were?"

"Let's see. Yea, I remember a few of them. Uh, the first few are easy. Awakening the soul. Liberating the spirit. Illuminating the path and um, let's see, oh yea, transforming the mindset."

"So far so good," I encouraged him. "What about healing your wounds, and strengthening the bonds of fellowship?" I asked.

"Right, right. I wonder how it is that I could have forgotten my *two favorites*," he smirked as he shot me one of his looks. "Let's see, the last one was, um, the rhythm of life, at least I think that was the last one."

"Well, that's not too bad. But knowing what they are is one thing. Making them a part of your life is something else. Where have you gotten with that?"

He was silent for a few minutes as he gathered his thoughts. "Well, overall, I feel pretty good about where I'm at. Although I'm finishing up with seeing you, I know that I have a long way to go with each of those steps. But I can see in more global terms how far I have come."

"What do you mean by global terms?" I wondered out loud.

"For example, I remember only too well what you told me when we started. It really pissed me off at the time, mostly because you were right about me, even more because you were right about the way this would all unfold."

"What do you mean?" I asked somewhat puzzled.

"You know that stuff about making this my work, not doing this to get somebody else off my back. In fact, I think your exact words were, 'When are you going to stop making this your fiancee's therapy and start making it your own work?'

"I didn't like what you had to say, but I got your point. Unless I was willing to go through this for myself, I would never get anything out of it. Believe me, that was a big shift for me, to make this my own journey rather than trying to make other people happy.

"But something else you said had a lasting impact on me as well. Remember how you told me what I could expect out of the first few weeks? I was so insistent on wanting to know how long all of this was going to take."

"I remember that you wanted this over with before you even got started."

"Yea, yea, you kept telling me you understood how frightened I was, but all I could do is look at you like you were crazy. But the point I wanted to make was when you told me about the first twelve weeks.

"You told me that I would start feeling better after two weeks. I think the term you used was, um, *subjective distress?* You said that the fear, anxiety, the loneliness, and the hopelessness would lessen after the first two weeks. By week eight, the circumstances that brought me here would settle down and I would begin to feel even better by then. That by week 12, I would start asking myself why the hell am I coming to see this guy in the first place.

"I don't know what your point was, but what I took from that was that this work is easy to do when someone is hurting, but there is more to this work than merely alleviating the symptoms. If I wanted to go beyond merely seeking relief from my symptoms, if I wanted to change more than the circumstances through which my pain was being expressed, I would have to find something other than the immediate pain in my life to keep me going. I would have to find something deep within me to motivate myself to grow and change.

"What occurred to me, whether you intended this or not, was that I was going to have to make a commitment to myself for myself. And you know what I realized? I had never done that before and more importantly, if I were brutally honest about it, that thought scared the living daylights out of me.

"To make such a commitment to myself would mean that I would have to believe that I was worth such a commitment, that I deserved such a commitment. Believe me, it took more than twelve weeks to get to a place of feeling like I deserved anything."

"You're right!" I exclaimed, "those are pretty big global shifts."

"Yea, I think what you would say is that I learned how to *take ownership* of my journey. I learned to not hold everyone but myself responsible for my well-being.

"The way I see it, I had to start seeing who I was and how I affected the people in my life rather than stay so focused on what the world was doing to me. I had to start seeing how the things that I was doing, the ways I protected myself just didn't work for me any more.

"When I started here, I was angry at everybody for not understanding me, not caring about me. I can see now that I wouldn't let anybody care about me. I had made my work the center of my universe and pushed everyone else away.

"As I drifted further and further away from the people that mattered most to me, from the things that brought me fun and pleasure, I didn't realize it at the time, but I *lost myself.*

"I guess that's the biggest thing that I will leave here with, knowing all the ways I lose myself and how destructive that is for me. I have to remember how to hold onto myself if I am going to make my life work for me the way I want it to."

"Hold onto yourself?" I liked the sound of it but I didn't know exactly what he meant.

"Yea, that's become almost a mantra for me. *Hold onto myself.* What I've learned is how easily I lose myself. In my relationships. In my ambition. In my value system. In the choices I make. In the issues I leave unresolved with my fiancée. Every area of my life is full of potholes for me to fall into. Hell, forget fall into, sometimes I willingly dive headfirst into them, but the end result is, I become totally disconnected from myself."

I was genuinely impressed by the depth of understanding that my client was taking from our experience together. "Well that does sound important. So how do you *hold onto yourself* these days?"

"I work at it. I don't think I'm there yet. But I keep working at it. In fact, I can honestly say I still lose myself in a lot of crap more times than not.

"But, I know now how important my friends are to me. They keep me grounded, so I work at these relationships, even when the work is tedious or overwhelming or both.

"Secondly, I've only uncovered the tip of the iceberg about myself. But I have to keep peeling back the layers that hide me from myself and the world. I never realized how *not-present* I was in my life. I've made it a point of absolute commitment to keep doing the work that will enable more and more of myself to show up in my day-to-day life.

"Lastly, and don't ask me to explain this one because I don't have a handle on any of it yet. But spirituality, spirituality is a big part of me *holding onto myself.* I divorced myself from that part of me my whole life because religion turned me off.

"I've learned from you that this isn't about religion, it's about a relationship I have with a higher part of myself and some kind of higher power in the world. I get it in my head, I just don't know what that looks like in my life just yet.

"But I also know, that all of this doesn't have to make sense to me just yet, in fact it's likely that it never will make complete sense to me. It's only important that I'm moving in the direction that will enable me to make sense out of all of this little by little. For I've come to accept that I'm a work in progress rather than a project waiting to be completed."

I looked at him with a big smile on my face and said, "You take my breath away. It's easy to see that you've made this journey your own voyage, where you're *discovering* your way rather than expecting somebody to *teach* you their way."

That's the secret to all of this, *discovering* your way. *Discovering* your path. Forsaking the safety and security of somebody else's expectations, somebody else's methods. Your life can only be genuinely lived by you with the courage you have to forge your own path. Anything else is a cheap imitation of somebody else's vision. You don't have to settle for less than the path that enables you to step out of the shadows and [re]connect to your life's journey.

As we travel together throughout this book on our shared journey, I will introduce you to different phrases that I use. They can only be useful for you if you take the time to discover your own meaning of each phrase rather than settling for what I tell you they mean to me. It will be worth your while to take the time to think about these different phrases and the steps they articulate. What I am suggesting is for you to begin shaping your own meaning as to what these phrases hold for you.

As you begin to do this, remember, there is no one correct meaning that each phrase holds, there is only a continually unfolding, uniquely personal meaning for you. So let's start out with *Stepping Out of the Shadows*. What does that phrase mean to you. Go ahead and write down a short description. It will be fun for you to revisit your answers and notice how much they change as you grow and change. If you need more room to write, go ahead and use some paper and place it here with the rest of what you have written.

_____

_____

_____

_____

_____

_____

_____

_____

_____
_____
_____
_____
_____
_____
_____
_____
_____
_____
_____
_____
_____
_____
_____
_____
_____
_____
_____
_____
_____
_____
_____

Exploring the meaning of *Stepping Out of the Shadows* reminds me of a conversation I had with my friend Mary Jo. Mary Jo and I have been friends for twenty years. We have watched each other struggle and grow stronger from those struggles. We know how hard we both have tried to be true to our paths as well as what our lives have looked like when we were totally disconnected from our paths. She was in town on business a while ago. We talked to each other into the wee hours of the morning taking an inventory of what life has taught us. She shared with me the most important lesson that she has learned.

"The times I have abandoned my path, those were the times I became confused and disoriented. I can see how certain choices I had made were more about stopping my pain and silencing my fear rather than honoring my life's journey."

I thought about what she said for a moment. I was staring off into the distance, listening to the piano player playing *Killing Me Softly With His Song*. Finally I said, "It sounds like you're saying that there were times you chose the path of least resistance, whatever was expedient, but a path that inevitably caused you more suffering than the pain and fear you were trying to escape."

"Steve, that's exactly right! At the time I believed I was choosing the only means available for me to survive. When I chose mere survival, my life became frozen. Every step I took was encased with rigidity, caution, self-protection, and inevitably self-sabotage. Those were the times that fear and hopelessness permeated my emotional world. Confusion, bewilderment, they both coated my mind with a clouded sense of who I was, where I was headed.

"As the feeling of being trapped with nowhere to go overtook my whole being, I sank deeper and deeper into a routine that ensured my safety but stifled my growth."

Mary Jo paused for a moment to collect her thoughts. She was being careful not to misspeak. She sipped her coffee as she continued, "Think about it this way. I developed a routine that gave me one thing: safety. But the net result? The net result was that I abandoned my sense of adventure, my willingness to take risks. My life became sterile. It was stripped of the natural emotional ups-and-downs. As a result, I lost myself."

"You lost yourself?" My eyes were squinting, almost as if I was searching for something in the air that would help me understand what she was saying.

"I lost my connection, my connection with, with my humanness."

"Your humanness?"

"Yea, let's see. How can I...?" she stared at the ceiling searching for a way to explain herself. "My humanness, my humanness, well my emotional experiences, I guess is what I mean. Those things that make us all human. My hopes, my sorrow, my joy, my wounds, my pain. All of that, I was totally disconnected from.

"My world was black and white. There was no pain, but there was no joy. There was just a growing sense of apathy, an increasing sense of powerlessness.

"By dedicating my life to the avoidance of pain, I became numb to all of my life experiences. You see, it was this very process of avoidance, routine, and emotional numbness to my life experiences that deadened my soul.

"Ultimately, what I discovered is a very simple truism, we all need to get [re]connected with the path that leads us out of the shadows, and to turn away from the means we use to drown out our pain and fear."

PART 2

*A*wakening the Soul

This is the true joy of life,
the being used for a purpose
recognized by yourself as a mighty one;
and being thoroughly worn out
before you are thrown on the scrap heap;
the being a force of nature
instead of a feverish little clod
of ailments and grievances complaining
that the world will not devote itself
to making you happy.

-George Bernard Shaw

$\mathcal{A}$ Life of Accommodation or Inspiration?

A musician must make music, an artist must paint, a poet must write, if he is to be ultimately at peace with himself.

- Abraham Maslow

I asked the question more out of frustration than anything else. The answer I got meant little to me at the time, but it has stayed with me ever since, taking on deeper meaning to me as the years have gone by.

I was in ninth grade, returning on a bus with my teammates, having just played the last basketball game of the season. We had lost the game, as usual. With my coach sitting next to me, I was lost deep in my thoughts.

Like I said, I was more frustrated than anything else when I blurted out, "How the hell can you stand it?"

"Stand what?" my coached asked in a somewhat stunned voice.

"This losing. All the time. All we do is lose. And I don't see it getting any better in the next couple of years. How do you keep going on? How do you maintain your enthusiasm for your job, for the team, for what we're doing? Why do you keep on coaching?"

"Well, I guess, I guess I just don't see things quite the way you do."

He caught my curiosity with that response. "What do you mean by that?" I wondered out loud.

"Well, when I think about coaching the team I don't measure everything we do by our wins and losses."

"You don't. What the hell else matters?" I shot back, feeling somewhat unnerved by his cavalier attitude.

"There are plenty of reasons I coach you guys, the least of which is whether we win or lose basketball games," my coach responded in his usual matter-of-fact manner.

My voice became shrill as I asked, "What are you trying to do, mess with my head? Like what? Why else would you put all the time and effort into this if you weren't interested in winning basketball games?"

"Well, one thing I love is working with young kids. It means a lot to me that I can help shape who all of you are becoming.

"Secondly, I love sports. Always have, always will. This gives me an opportunity to stay active in a part of my life that has meant so much to me throughout the years."

Things were beginning to get a bit thick for me so I thought I would try and inject a note of reality into the discussion. "Yea coach, that's all well and good, but the truth of the matter is, we suck!"

"Listen, I understand how you may feel the way you do, but being a coach means more to me than just x's and o's. It means that I get to be myself for three hours a day for six days of the week.

"It's a time when I can get away from all the politics of being a teacher, get away from the demands of being a father and a husband, it's a time each day when I feel like I am doing what I was placed on this earth to do."

"Yelling and screaming, making us run laps? That's your life's calling?" I was beginning to regret ever starting this conversation.

"No, but giving to others, making a difference in somebody else's life, teaching you guys that there's more to life than sports and girls. Having a part of my life that's *play*, being part of the camaraderie that you have with any sports team, that's all very important to me. I find it all very rewarding."

"I don't know, when you're yelling at us all the time,

I never get the sense that you're feeling all that *rewarded*."

"That's my point exactly. Coaching sports is rewarding because it lets me live my life in a way that matters to me. Just because I get frustrated, doesn't mean I feel like coaching isn't rewarding. In fact, figuring out how to overcome the things that are frustrating me is a part of why coaching is so rewarding.

"That's why I see winning and losing as a small part of all of this. When I think about us as a team, I think about our squad over the long haul. The outcome of each game is just a marker of where we are and what we have to do next to wind up where we eventually want to be.

"Staying true to that is more important to me than our won-lost record. I guess I'm trying to say a couple of different things to you. Number one, I keep doing this because of the personal satisfaction I get from doing it. I don't know how else to explain that to you. It's just something that I believe I was meant to do with my life. I'm happiest when I'm doing things in my life that I was meant to be doing.

"Number two, I keep coaching because coaching allows me to keep growing.

"You ask me how it is I continue. It's simple. What else would I do? Where else would I go? I don't make my choices based upon what would alleviate my frustration or how best to avoid frustrating situations.

"I take whoever I am with me wherever I go. If I'm not true to who I am, I will never be able to escape *that frustration*. So I make my life choices based upon what situation is the best arena for me to use my innate talents and interests, not what would be the least frustrating for me.

"All the losses don't discourage me from continuing,

because you see, coaching is *what I do,* but it isn't *who I am.* Coaching is the vehicle that enables me to be who I am."

I wasn't able to understand it at the time, but my coach was sharing with me his formula for a life of well-being that was built upon his life-choices, life-choices that were a reflection of who he was, his abilities, his interests, his passions, his desire to contribute to other people's well-being.

He was teaching me about his value system, a value system different than the one I used to evaluate myself and the events of my life. His message was a simple one, although I didn't understand it at the time. He was encouraging me not to measure myself by such things as whether you win or lose, make a lot of money or don't, have a prestigious job or not.

No, he clearly understood something very important. He understood that there was a much more important benchmark to use when we evaluate ourselves, the decisions we make about our lives, how we live our lives, and the basis for the choices we make.

That benchmark? Well I see it more clearly now than back then. Quite simply, our life-choices are a reflection of our soul.

I never had considered that there would be more to measuring my life. It would be very dramatic to tell you that single conversation made a profound difference in my life, but the truth is, that conversation wasn't an eye opener at that point in my life. As I said earlier, looking back, I could see it was a beginning, a beginning that took years to bear any fruit.

In my coach's day, he would say, "I'm just doing what

makes me happiest." How I think about what my coach did was create his own path, a path by which he could [re]connect to his life's journey. And there are specific steps we all need to take in order to [re]connect to our life's journey.

The first step to [re]connecting to our life's journey, is what I refer to it as *Awakening the Soul*. Let me first ask you, what exactly does that phrase mean to you, *Awakening the Soul*?

- ❀Awakening the deeply buried, hidden parts of who we are?
- ❀Awakening the unused potential that lives within each and everyone of us?
- ❀Awakening those parts of ourselves longing to be given a voice?
- ❀Awakening the longings for a life that reflects who we genuinely are?
- ❀Awakening the stirrings that have been anesthetized by the judgments and expectations of others?
- ❀Awakening the courage that has been cowered by our own high expectations?
- ❀Awakening the essence of who we are?

Does any of that fit for you? Perhaps you have your own ideas about what *Awakening the Soul* means to you. Why not write a short description of what *Awakening the Soul* means to you?

_____

_____

_____

_____

_____
_____
_____
_____
_____
_____
_____
_____
_____
_____
_____
_____
_____
_____
_____
_____
_____
_____
_____

Whatever *Awakening the Soul* means to you, make no mistake about this basic point. We will remain in limbo until we go through a process of awakening. Awakening to who we are by integrating our disowned parts. Awakening to what is important to us by creating a life that reflects our newly created whole self. Awakening to the connection between our life's journey and living a purposeful life.

Come Out, Come Out, Wherever You Are!

*Our greatest pretenses are built up not to hide
the evil and the ugly in us, but our emptiness. The
hardest thing to hide is something that is not there.*

-Eric Hofer

Just what is it that our souls have been buried under? What has so anesthetized our soul? What is it that leaves us disconnected from the very essence of who we are?

Well, there are volumes of books written on the subject, so it would be hard to distill all of that into a mere chapter, but let me see if you recognize this about yourself.

Paula's story is one of the classic ugly duckling who turned into a swan. We shared a couple of classes together in grad school. We would often work on projects together, so we spent a lot of time with each other. One night over coffee, Paula told me about herself and the obstacles that had shaped her into who she was today.

"Knowing me now, you would have never guessed what it was like for me growing up. I was short and chubby until I was fourteen. My mom made me cut my hair really short. I wore a pair of glasses that were from hell."

"Ech!" we laughed together.

"Need I tell you that I was the object of everybody's ridicule? It was really merciless."

"I had only one seemingly saving grace, how well I did at school. Now, that was the only thing that saved me from being totally ostracized by the kids my age.

"Don't get me wrong. I never kidded myself. I knew what few friends I did have liked me only so that I could help them with their homework."

"Well, how did all of that change for you?" I asked, not able to match the person I knew today with the person in the scenario from back then.

"A funny thing happened to me. I don't know what it

was, maybe my hormones finally kicked in. I grew some, shed my baby fat, convinced my mom to let me change my hair style and get contacts.

"Overnight, the very people who had taunted me began to embrace me. The only problem with dating became who was I going to choose. I continued to excel in school. I had gone from being the butt of everyone's joke, having my name painted on the bathroom walls, being shunned by everybody because of my physical appearance to the homecoming queen."

"Wow, that must have been sweet revenge," I said. The odd thing was, she didn't agree with me. In fact, she started sobbing.

"I can't tell you how much hell all of that was for me. And it haunts me to this very day."

"What do you mean?" I asked, feeling somewhat embarrassed for not understanding any of this at all.

"Don't you see? Look, when everyone was making fun of me, it was because of how I looked. The only reason anyone liked me at all was because of what I could do.

"Then all of a sudden my looks became more acceptable and people liked me for what I looked like as well as what I could do.

"The point is I never was liked or disliked for who I was. Me on the inside never impacted anybody. I never learned to know *me* much less value *me*. When I was too ugly, I hated *me* because of my appearance. When I became attractive in everyone's mind, well there you had it, it just reinforced that my value was derived from my physical appearance.

"But all along, there was a whole *me* buried deep inside myself. Never coming out, never daring to show her *face*. This part of *me* stayed hidden from myself and the world."

I tried putting this together. "So you never really built your life based upon who you were, you just figured that people would like you for what you could do and how you looked?"

"Sorta. I mean I put doing and achieving above all else, above just being. I viewed everything as a competition where if I didn't win, I was a loser. I never had any satisfaction from what I accomplished. It was like there was a black hole inside of me that never could be filled."

"What would happen to you if you were to become less achievement oriented?" I asked her.

"I don't know. What pops into my head is, I would lose myself. I would be totally lost, I would have no sense of myself."

We sat quietly for awhile trying to absorb all that we had just discussed. Looking at Paula's face, I could see that she had reopened some painful memories.

For me, I was more confused than anything. I just couldn't connect the person I knew today with the person Paula was describing. I somehow felt responsible for not being sensitive enough to what Paula was going through.

After a few more moments, Paula wiped her eyes, then gently layed her hand upon mine, as if to say she understood how hard this was for me to see her so upset.

Then she continued, "The moral of the story is I had built my life on a never ending treadmill chasing affirmation, acceptance, and self-worth through other people's recognition of my appearance as well as my accomplishments. But the point is, I had never found a way to provide love and affirmation for myself about myself. I was completely estranged from myself, unable to ever do enough or be enough to fill that void."

We all recognize the pact that Paula made with herself. It sounds something like this, "In order for me to be accepted, in order for me to fit in, I will forfeit all of who I am."

Do you understand what I mean by *forfeiting who we are?* We shut off, tune out, disconnect from who we really are. The sense of importance we place upon other people accepting us becomes so out of proportion that we lose ourselves.

Just what is it that we lose when we make this kind of pact? Inevitably, we sacrifice our whole emotional being. In order to conform, in order to please, in order to pursue what others deem important for us to be, we have only one choice: we disconnect from our emotions.

Why is this divorce, the divorcing of our emotions from our soul, such an inevitable outcome? Quite simply, our emotions, our feelings are little more than the manifestation of our passions, our passions being the manifestation of what is important to us.

Our emotions are a sign post. They are an affirmation of the path we are on, the people we are with, the destiny we are chasing. When things are clicking, when things are in sync, we know it by what our feelings are telling us. When things are present in our life in a way that does not honor who we are, our emotions tell us that as well.

To sustain a life in which our soul is not connected to what we're doing, who we're becoming, we must learn to ignore our whole emotional-self.

Our emotions will let us know whether something is

right or wrong for us. When we choose to ignore what our emotions are telling us, we set ourselves up to be hurt. Think about the person who stays in an abusive relationship. Or how about the person stuck in a job that may be financially rewarding but not a reflection of that person's interests and talents? What about the people who forsake their personal life by burying themselves in their work? In order to sustain a life with that many contradictions between who we genuinely are and what we have in our lives, we must learn to ignore our emotions or deaden them in any variety of ways.

The second part that we disconnect from ourselves is the little voice inside of us. The voice that guides us as we make choices. The voice that is connected to our soul. Some people may think of it as intuition.

Now don't be put off by my choice of words. I don't mean to insinuate that there is some paranormal experience taking place. I am only describing a phenomena that we all experience. Our little voice is the guide we learn to trust, to listen to when we are living our lives from inside of ourselves. You see, that little voice is the direct link between who we are and how who we are gets injected into our lives.

When we are [re]connected to our life's journey, our little voice is honored as we clean out the parts of our life that do not match who we are. Our little voice is followed when we make decisions on what direction our life should take.

However, when we make the kind of pact that puts other people's opinions and judgments ahead of our own, we stop heeding our inner voice or we shut it off all together.

But let's slow things down for a moment. This would be a good time to stop and reflect upon what I've just gone over. Does anything I have just examined hold any relevance for you? Have you made any pacts that have led to you disconnecting from your soul? If so what are the pacts?

_____

_____

_____

_____

_____

_____

_____

_____

_____

_____

_____

What have you had to sacrifice about who you are in order to make and sustain these pacts?

_____

_____

_____

_____

_____

_____

_____

_____

_____

_____

_____

_____

_____

_____

_____

_____

We not only lose ourselves by forfeiting who we are or disconnecting from the little voice inside, we oftentimes become overwhelmed to the point of being paralyzed by the wounds that we carry around inside of us. What is it that paralyzes us, paralyzes us to the point that we hide? We hide who we are, we hide what we feel. We hide what matters to us.

Johnny is a close friend of mine. I've watched Johnny wrestle with himself over the years. His life was out of control because he wasn't connected to his soul. He had abandoned his soul at a very early age. Abandoned it so he wouldn't have to feel the pain of betrayal. Abandoned it so that he wouldn't feel so consumed by the confusion he felt. Abandoned it in order that he might simply survive.

Johnny survived by building a shell. A shell around his wounds. A shell that separated the world from himself. Sadly, a shell that separated Johnny from Johnny.

Johnny has fought long and hard to awaken the parts of himself that he had buried out of sight. As a result of his courageous work, he has found a way to be present in his life. Present to the people he knows and the circumstances he faces. Today he enjoys a life free from panic and fear. Especially paniced that he would be found out for who he feared that he was.

You see, Johnny lived in fear of anybody finding out, finding _him_ out. And he coped with that fear by totally disconnecting, thereby deadening his soul.

He learned at a very early age how to finesse the people in his life. For him, it was a matter of survival. He didn't see it any other way.

Survival to him meant never letting anybody find out. Never letting them find out his secret.

So how could he possibly let the world get close? How could he run the risk of anybody getting close enough to see? See his doubts. See his confusion. See the guilt that paralyzed him. How could he possibly share the doubts he carried around about himself?

No, the only way for him to cope was to create pseudo-intimacy with the people in his life. He knew all the right things to say. He knew when to say them. He knew as long as he kept feeding them what they wanted to hear, they would never go looking for who he truly was.

The only problem was the longer he hid who he was, the more shame he felt about who he was. The cycle became more and more vicious. The more shame he felt about who he was, the more he drank. The more he drank, the more he slid into his private world: a world racked with shame, fear, confusion, and secrecy.

Now, not only was he running from his past, he had to hide his present as well. But, he convinced himself that was the only way to survive.

Afterall, that's how he survived throughout his whole childhood. Unable to trust anybody. Unable to feel cared about by anybody. Unable to feel safe with another person. He just invented a new life. A life that was separate from what was going on inside of him.

And at the age of thirty, he was still doing the same thing. Living a double life. A life where he played at being whole. He played at being involved. He played at being connected with the people in his life.

But the longer this double life went on, the worse his drinking and drugging became. The worse his acting out became. The more shame he felt about his secret life, the more out of control his public life became.

Women. They would leave just as quickly as they came. Jobs. He had been fired from three in the last two years. He would go through periods of being estranged from his family. There were times when he was one step ahead of the bill collector, but that didn't keep him from getting more credit cards and maxing them out. His friendships seemed to end abruptly in fits of anger and disappointment, never to be repaired.

But he could fool you. From the outside looking in, you would never have guessed. You would never have guessed at the emotional swirl that was going on within him. You would have never guessed how fear consumed his every waking moment.

You would have never guessed how much pure panic permeated his emotional world. And it all got acted out so that he could hide, hide from himself and the world around him.

In fact, it seemed that initiating a new relationship was the precipitant of the cycle repeating itself, always ending in tears and accusations. The more women he brought into his life, the more he acted out. Everything became out of control as he had to maintain this double life until finally he went to get help for himself, finally reconnecting to his soul by shedding the shell he had created to hide his wounds.

For many of us, disconnecting from our soul has

been a means of coping. Coping with the well of pain, coping with the well of fear that has consumed us our whole lives. The cause of the fear and pain may differ from person to person, but the means of coping looks the same. We all have secrets. We all have our ways of hiding what we don't want the world to know about us. We all inevitably hide parts of our soul so that we aren't found out.

We believe we have to hide ourselves from ourselves and the world. The solution: invent a new person. So we go about the business of divorcing ourselves from who we are by creating somebody we believe the world wants us to be. The more we crawl into this shell, the more convinced we become about how unacceptable the core of who we are actually is.

This just keeps the cycle going. The paradox that allowed us to initially survive becomes the means by which our soul becomes emotionally and spiritually deadened. After awhile, we're no longer hiding the pain and shame that we feel about ourselves, we're only hiding the fact of how empty we feel inside, how empty our lives have become.

The solution to ending this cycle is using the courage we all possess, the courage to discard the shell we have created. The act of discarding our outer shell will make room for the emergence of our awakening soul. As we make room for those parts of ourselves that have lived in slumber our whole lives, we will experience our lives taking a new direction, a direction that enables us to step out of the shadows.

Let's stop for a moment and think about the parts of yourself that you leave buried deep inside of you. For example, there may be a part of you hungering to be loved by somebody special but too afraid to let anyone else know that part exists inside of you. Or there may be a part of you who feels very angry for always being taken advantage of by other people, but too scared to let anyone know how angry you are. Or a part of you that is kind and gentle but doesn't feel safe expressing that kindness for fear that your kindness will be taken advantaged of. Or a creative part of you may want to be an actor but is frightened of disappointing your parents if you don't become the executive that they want you to be.

Whatever the part(s) that you are aware of that are hidden away, let's see if you can first identify what they are.

_____

_____

_____

_____

_____

_____

Next, for each part you have identified, what is so frightening about bringing that part more consistently into your life?

_____

_____

_____

_____

_____

_____

_____

_____

_____

_____

_____

_____

_____

_____

_____

_____

_____

_____

_____

_____

_____

_____

_____

_____

_____

_____

_____

_____

_____

The point is we all have good reasons for disconnecting from our souls. The means by which we disconnect may differ but the result is the same. We bury alive essential parts of who we are. Without these essential parts, we are less than whole. In burying any part of who we are, we have chosen to keep part of ourselves in the shadows. By [re]connecting to our life's journey, we will discover ways to escape the shadows by bringing all of who we are to the table.

*A*wakening: Questioning or Examining?

The truth is that all of us attain the greatest success and happiness possible in this life whenever we use our native capacities to their greatest extent.

-Dr. Smiley Blanton

So what is it that we have become disconnected from within ourselves? What is it that we are seeking to awaken, seeking to become [re]connected to again?

As part of my own searching, I have befriended many people throughout the years. Friends who have walked their own path. Friends who know the pain of being disconnected from their life's journey. Friends who have found their way back.

I have tried to tap into the wisdom that lives within them. Wisdom born out of their own trials and tribulations. Wisdom born out of the lessons taught when we surrender our willful, ego-based solutions for the solutions that are born from our soul.

One such friend is a mentor of mine, good ol' Marty. Marty has worked in halfway houses for over twenty-five years. Believe me when I tell you, Marty has seen it all, whether it be the trials and tribulations of his own journey or the wrestling matches others have engaged in trying to discover how to [re]connect to their own journey.

Early on in my own searching, I had a discussion with Marty about this step, *Awakening the Soul.* We were both at a weekend retreat and had taken a walk in the woods. We came upon a small lake, so we sat down and talked about some ideas I had been chewing on.

Marty was chewing on a blade of grass, mindlessly tossing pebbles into the lake when he turned to me and said, "You're absolutely right. There is an awakening that we all must experience. Whatever you call that which awakens is merely a matter of semantics.

"I think of it as my true authentic self. I believe it's the part of me that has lived and will continue to live throughout eternity. It's the part of me that is tapped into the collective unconscious of our universe."

"Huh? What!" I sensed a familiar cloud of frustration and confusion coming over me.

Marty cautioned me, "Try not to listen to me with your head. Listen for a moment with your heart. Listen with your mind's eye, watch where my words take you. Pay attention to the images evoked by what I am telling you. Most importantly, be patient.

"My true authentic self or soul or whatever it is that you want to call it, well I think of it as a quality of myself, ummm, how can I say this, a quality of myself that lives deep beneath the complexity of my personality."

Marty paused for a moment and watched me. He gently placed a hand on my shoulder, trying to reassure me. He told me to close my eyes as I listened, to only pay attention to my breathing. "Just let my words in. Watch how your body begins to embrace an idea long before your mind does. Watch, learn, take notice of how your body reacts to what I'm saying. You see, that's where our awakening begins.

"My soul, well for me, how I understand it, my soul is the part of myself buried beneath my belief system and attitudes. Those two little buddies of mine—my beliefs and attitudes—are simply a lot of noise that goes on in my head, noise that most often drowns out the voice through which my soul speaks to me. Quite simply, my soul is like a reservoir, a reservoir of inner wisdom that guides my life."

I was trying to digest all that he had just said. His words had been reassuring, yet at the same time, I was even more confused by it all. I began nervously throwing rocks in the lake.

Marty let me wrestle with all of what he had just said for at least a good half-hour. He sat silently on a rock as the mist began to rise off the lake. The smell of late autumn was in the air as we took in the afternoon sun.

Finally, I returned to him and said, "You know, that's what's hardest for me. I see how your life is the embodiment of having embraced the spirit of what you just said, yet, I can barely make any sense out of it."

He must have noticed the hurt etched in my face. He searched for something reassuring to say. He gave me a kind look as he said, "That's just as it should be. We all wrestle with trying to *understand* when what we only need to be doing is *embracing*.

"My rule of thumb is if you find yourself struggling to *understand*, it only means you're not ready to *embrace* some aspect of where you are in your journey. There's some fear or some part of your will that is holding on for dear life."

"What do you mean by that?" I asked. I had honestly never considered that I was holding onto something I wasn't ready to let go of.

"Can't you see how your intellect, your insistence on understanding all that's not immediately observable to you is merely a defense against embracing all that's not immediately observable to you."

"A defense against embracing it?" I was lost.

"Sure, our fears, our insecurities. All those things that insist that we understand our path before we can embrace it. All those things that insist that we understand in order for us to connect to that path. All those things that insist that the limit of our understanding must be defined by the limits of what we can perceive with our eyes or our mind."

Marty chuckled to himself as he continued, "Let me ask you, when you're a passenger in a car, do you let the driver drive or are you constantly telling the driver what to do? In fact, you don't have to tell me the answer to that question, I can only imagine what you're like."

A self-conscious smile broke out on my face. "Heh, should I just sit there in silence if I know a better way?"

"Well, let's see if you can get my point. The more you insist on understanding the ins and outs of your life's journey, the more you're like a back-seat driver in a car.

"You see, our soul is driving our lives. We're the one's that keep screwing the ride up. We make the journey longer than it need be, choppier than it need be, more painful than it need be. We may think we know a better direction to take but until we learn to tap into our soul, we're merely spinning our wheels."

"Okay, okay, I get your point. I don't need to figure out what all this means. But let me ask you, what do you mean by tapping into my soul?"

"We all need to learn how to access that little voice within ourselves. That little voice that we can turn to when we need to know whatever choice we're about to make is for our higher good."

"Higher good?" I asked him.

"Yes, higher good. Are we making choices that honor who we are or are we making choices to appease our little gods?"

"I know I'm not supposed to try and understand all of this, but what do you mean by little gods?"

"Little gods? Oh that's just a saying I use. I simply mean the gods we pay so much honor to, the gods for which we forsake the voice of our soul. Fear. Shame. Will. Ego. Control. Prestige. Power. Self-aggrandizement. Ambivalence. Egocentricity. Caution. Taking the easy way out. Insecurity. Those are all our little gods."

"So like anything else, awakening our soul boils down to the choices we make?"

Marty shook his head in agreement as he said, "Well, yea, I suppose so, in certain respects. Honor ourselves or appease the little gods, yea that's a choice.

"Look at the choices we have made throughout our lives, choices that have anesthetized our soul through the use of drugs and alcohol, through the hopelessness of depression and the anxiety from our fear, through the self-loathing of shame and self-alienation, and through the pain of loneliness and despair. Anger and resentment may have so twisted our spirit that we have ceased to believe our life can be any different."

"Just how do people climb out of that hole of despair and discouragement?" I wondered out loud.

"Just as you say, making a choice, a choice to awaken our soul is the antidote to becoming disconnected from the true purpose of our life's journey. A purpose that leaves us connected to ourselves, our community of fellowship, and our higher power."

We talked well into the night but finally the chill of the evening chased us inside. That night I stayed up late pondering what we had discussed. There was a rush of excitement that ran through my body. I didn't feel like I understood anything any better but I felt like finally someone had given me something to sink my teeth into.

I felt like I finally had some direction to focus my attention. I didn't know where it would take me but I felt a little more grounded than I had been feeling up to that point.

Embarking on the Search

*Regret for the things that we did can be
tempered by time; it is regret for the things we did
not do that is inconsolable.*

-Sydney J. Harris

Pathfinder's Tip

*Our soul will awaken when we forsake questioning our
journey for embracing our journey.*

What's the struggle behind the quest for understanding? What's the hidden drama that's going on behind
the curtain of our mind, the drama about *understanding* our journey rather than *embracing* it. What are we
so damned afraid of? What are we so unwilling to
let go of?

Could it be true that our need to understand everything actually gets in the way of our ability to embrace a
new path?

Well, I have thought about this one for a long time.
The more I focus on this question, the more aware I
become of all the conditions we create before we give
ourselves to an experience.

Do you understand what I mean by *giving ourselves to
an experience?*

Paul's a friend of mine who's in a twelve-step program.
He works a program, you might say, almost fanatically.
But it wasn't always that way for him. I remember him
describing the slow gradual shift that took place for him.

Paul had a sheepish grin on his face as he said, "I went
through sponsors quicker than Sherman went through
Atlanta. They fired me time and time again because I
wouldn't listen."

"You're stubbornness got in the way?" I asked.

"Stubbornness, yea, I suppose it looks that way from the outside. I know I can be stubborn, but this was more than being muleheaded. It's just that everything that was suggested to me seemed to come out of left field. It was like I was told to throw away everything but the kitchen sink in terms of thinking about who I was and how I should live my life.

"It was more confusing than anything else. Believe me, I wanted my program to work, but man, it was scary, it was downright scary to have to make all of those changes."

"It sounds like you were holding on for dear life for awhile," I offered.

"Holding on, yea—with my fingernails. I was kicking and screaming, resisting going to the places these guys wanted me to go to. Holding on, you bet I was, I was desperately trying to hold onto myself.

"This may seem weird to you but I felt like if I just blindly followed what I was told to do, that I would melt away, kinda like the wicked witch in the *Wizard of Oz*. It honestly seemed that I would evaporate into nothingness. I wasn't so much fighting my sponsors, it was just the only way I knew to keep *me*.

"Do you have any idea how scary it is to grow out of your very skin? Man, what they were telling me to do, well, it was like, like they were trying to make me start to live my life left-handed after thirty years of living right-handed. Where is me in all of that?"

"So you're saying you weren't really being stubborn as much as you were trying to preserve yourself, your sense of who you were, your way of life?" I asked Paul.

"Bingo. That's exactly it. It wasn't so much what my sponsors were suggesting, it wasn't what the books were suggesting, it was where this runaway train was headed, everything felt out of control, so I did the only thing I knew how to do, I decided to dig in. Dig in to slow things down, dig in to feel in control, dig in for self-preservation.

"And I did it the only way I knew how, I fought them tooth and nail on everything. I questioned everything. I needed an explanation for everything that they suggested I do. Why do I have to call you so much? Why do I have to read this book? What the hell is a higher power and how do you turn *it* over to *him?*

"Listen, if I was going to turn myself inside out, I wanted some damn good reasons for doing it."

"Looking back I see it a little more clearly. But I approached things like I had to be an expert on something new before I would ever try it. The result was I never had to try anything because I was too busy learning about it."

"Well, you must have gotten the answers you were looking for, because look at how things are now!" I remarked somewhat admiringly.

"Not at all. You're not getting my point. All that I got originally for all of my questioning and stubbornness was bounced around. In fact, I took myself further and further away from where I am today rather than closer.

"No, the harder I tried holding on, the more I questioned things and tried to understand them, the more bogged down I became. In fact, I began to question whether the program was right for me, after all it hadn't done a damn thing for me."

"That changed for you?" I asked somewhat perplexed by his winding and twisting path.

"At some point I realized that the program wasn't suppose to do anything for me, that I was suppose to *give myself to it.*"

"You mean kinda of like being a Steppford wife, you just kinda mindlessly go through life like a puppet without a mind of your own?"

"No, just the opposite, I had to develop my mind more than ever. Questioning wasn't using my mind. It was just having a knee-jerk reaction to everything I encountered. No, I decided to use my mind alright—I stopped questioning and began searching."

"What the hell is the difference?" I asked, not getting any of this at all.

"The difference between questioning and searching—you mean that isn't as obvious as the nose on your face?" Paul chuckled.

I just shrugged my shoulders.

"Questioning and searching, let's see, the difference between the two, well, how about it depends upon what part of your soul the act is coming from."

I frowned at Paul, not feeling the least bit comforted by this explanation.

"What I learned was when I was questioning, I was merely digging my feet in. I was coming from a place in my depths called fear. Fear of letting go, fear of losing all that was familiar to me and about me. Fear of not measuring up. And most profoundly, frightened of becoming so vulnerable, frightened of living life without all the ways I kept myself safe, no matter how much harm that brought me.

"The way I picture it in my mind is my questioning was a means of grasping. Kinda like being in a hurricane with the wind blowing 150 mph. My questioning was my way of clinging to the last standing tree, believing that if I were to stop my questioning, I would be blown away with everything else."

"Okay, Paul, so we're basically talking survival here."

"Yea, it was in my mind, no question about it, it was about survival for me."

"All right, I get that, but what about this other thing, 'searching,' I think you said? What about searching and the part of the soul that searching comes from?"

"Um, I was afraid you were going to ask me that. Let's see, searching, does searching and trust go together? Searching and, well, I guess faith is in there somewhere as well. Trusting yourself, your path, the people who you have invited on your journey, I dunno, there's probably something about surrender in there to.

"Searching for me is like, like a willingness. A willingness to discover what is *so* about myself, that is what is the truth about my path, my life's journey. It's kinda like being *open to*.

"At least that's what searching is for me. Questioning allowed me to dig in, searching empowered me to reclaim from within myself that which is sacred and liberating about who I am.

"Searching, that is an act of discrimination. You know kinda like being able to sort out what is useful for my life and what is not. Searching let's me tap into the wisdom of mankind, sifting, sorting, trying on what I like and discarding what doesn't feel right for me.

"Ultimately, searching led me to being more honest with myself.

"Again, I can only tell you what it looks like in my

mind. It's the difference between driving a car with one finger on the steering wheel or both hands clenched furiously to the steering wheel.

"When I began searching rather than questioning, I realized I started to examine myself rather than question the way I searched. I became more open to the fact that this journey was about who I was rather than how well I performed on it."

"Okay. I can get behind that, but, it seems to me, Paul, that something must have shifted inside of you as well. It seems like when you were questioning, you lived in an energy that was clutching at, holding onto, that everything was fear based."

"Yea, I suppose you're right. The shift, well let's see, I suppose what shifted for me was, um, well, how about I went from fighting to accepting, the difference in energy between those two. I stopped fighting everything and everyone and started accepting.

"Not everything, by any stretch of the imagination, but little by little I am gradually learning to accept things more.

Let me propose a concrete way to think about the path that Paul walked. In a word, surrender. Surrendering your will. Surrender is a part of any system of transformation. There's no getting around this simple fact. At this stage of the game, there's a part of us that's more intent on holding onto rather than surrendering. This conflict between our will clinging to all that is familiar, rather than surrendering to the steps that remove us from all that is familiar, creates an incredible amount of drama in our lives. It's this very drama that prolongs our slumber, that prevents our awakening from occurring. Yet it's this very drama that offers us many lessons about who we are and the life we are living.

So let's take a moment and examine how this drama is a part of your life. How does the drama created from the refusal of your will to surrender appear in your life? What does that drama look like when it appears in your life?

_____

_____

_____

_____

_____

_____

_____

_____

_____

_____

_____

What's the fear you have if you were to surrender, to let go of the familiar for the path of the unknown? What do you fear will happen to you?

_____

_____

_____

_____

_____

_____

_____

_____

How can your life be better served by surrendering your will to a path of awakening?

_____

_____

_____

_____

_____

_____

_____

_____

_____

_____

_____

_____

_____

_____

_____

I hope the curtain is being raised a little. I hope you're beginning to get glimpses of the Truth Paul eventually discovered for himself. Paul discovered what we all need to discover for ourselves. The truth about fear. You see fear, fear is the impediment. It's the immovable object. It's the boulder in our path. Do we avoid it? Go around it? Be stopped by it? Or go through it? Well, what I believe is that the only way out is through and so we need only find a way to go through our fear.

The benefit? Movement. [Re]connecting. Growth.

The solution? Letting go of our insistence on under-standing, discovering the ways that we can embrace our life's journey.

Bringing Honor to the Journey

*Every creator painfully experiences
the chasm between his inner vision
and its ultimate expression.*

-Issac Bashevis Singer

Pathfinder's Tip

*Our soul will awaken when we choose to honor ourselves
rather than appease our little gods.*

Honoring ourselves or appeasing the little gods.
Honoring ourselves? Just what is the act of honoring ourselves? What does it look like? What does it involve? How
does it take place?

What are these little gods that we abandon ourselves
to? What is the power they hold over us? What is the fear
that so paralyzes us that we choose to continue our relationship with them rather than forge a different kind of
relationship with ourselves?

Well, let's start with the little gods. By what names are
they known to us? How do they appear in our lives?

🐾 Control
🐾 Egoism
🐾 Caution
🐾 Willfulness
🐾 Perfectionism
🐾 Right vs. wrong
🐾 Competitiveness
🐾 Self-centeredness
🐾 Fear of the unknown
🐾 Avoidance of pain

To better understand the choices we make, it's important to recognize how we pay homage to our little gods rather than honor ourselves. Once we see how we forsake our soul for these little gods, we can free ourselves to listen to our soul and find the things necessary within ourselves to honor our soul. Take some time and look within yourself.

What are the names of your little gods? What is the power they hold over you?

_____

_____

_____

_____

_____

_____

_____

_____

_____

_____

_____

_____

_____

_____

_____

_____

_____

_____

_____

_____

As we become more aware of what our little gods are, we need next learn about the ways these little gods appear in our life, the ways these little gods chip away at our emotional and spiritual well-being. So take some time to tease out how such little gods like *perfectionism, willfulness,* and others appear in and impact your life.

_____

_____

_____

_____

_____

_____

_____

_____

_____

_____

_____

_____

_____

_____

_____

_____

_____

_____

_____

_____

_____

_____

_____

_____

_____

_____

The flip side of this? Honoring ourselves? Being true to who we are? Be all that you can be? Do these sayings have meaning to you or are they just overused clichés? Just what does honoring ourselves mean, more importantly what does it look like in our day-to-day lives?

Laura has been helping me with those very questions, sharing with me what it looks like for her, giving me glimpses of what it might be for me.

"I feel like I woke up one day and asked myself, 'Where did I disappear to?'"

"You mean, like you were missing in action?"

Laura chuckled and said, "Yea, in a manner of speaking, I guess you could put it that way.

"For whatever reason, I just came to realize that I had literally abandoned myself. Abandoned my interests, my passions, all the things that brought me joy, they were no longer a part of me, a part of my life."

"Life has a way of doing that to us," I offered.

"This wasn't life, this was me doing it to me. I just lost, well no, it wasn't interest, it was more like I lost touch, I lost touch with all those things that made living life more of a celebration rather than a test of survival."

"The books I used to read, the walks along the lake every evening, my arts and crafts projects, the long talks with my friends, there were so many ways I used to express myself, so many ways I used to be involved with people, with life. Gone. It all just stopped."

"You know, now that you mention it, I remember how we used to talk about the music you were writing, but I haven't heard much about that anymore."

"That's my point, but much worse than that was all the ways I was hurting myself. That was a whole different way that I would abandon myself. All the choices I made, all the ways I was sabotaging myself. I have so much shame about how out-of-control my life became.

"But..." I tried to get out a word of understanding.

"But nothing. I did things that just had no integrity to them. Those things cling to me like sludge from a black lagoon."

"Wow, those things still seem to cut real deep for you."

"Yea, they do. So much waste, so much lost potential. And for what? Such a long time to go without me. So long to go without: without my dignity, my joy, my passions. I gave it all away, and sadly enough, I gave it all away so cheaply."

The pain that was etched on her face reminded me of the pain I once saw on a mother who had to bury her two year old son.

I was moved by Laura's profound sense of loss. But at the same time there was some sort of transformation that came over her. So much pain yet at the same time it seemed she was experiencing some sort of emancipation. It was as if revisiting her pain was enabling her to reclaim a part of who she was. It seemed as if the bitterness was melting into gratitude right before my very eyes.

I was only guessing, but perhaps gratitude for the opportunity to grow, maybe for the opportunity to complete something within her, or gratitude for the opportunity to learn something new about herself, I didn't really know.

But what I took away from that conversation has made me think long and hard about what it means to honor ourselves. And what the connection between honoring ourselves and awakening our soul is.

Honoring ourselves is a two-step process. The first step is reclaiming. We need to reclaim the parts of ourselves that we have denied, pushed away, or cast aside. In order to honor ourselves, we need to reclaim what is rightfully ours, the good, the bad, and the ugly. Our emotional experiences, we need to reclaim our passions, all the ways we express who we are to the world.

Reclaiming. It's an act of ownership. It's an act of courage, an act of living your life in spite of the consequences of what that may bring to you rather than carving out a life where you are what you believe the world wants you to be.

Once we reclaim these pieces, we need next consistently give expression to all the parts of who we are. We need to express them, and more importantly refine them, add to them, consolidate them.

The connection to an awakening soul? Simple. You see, honoring ourselves is active, not passive. It's not something to be learned about, it's something we do.

Let's end this section with an opportunity for you to identify parts of yourself that you long ago abandoned. What are the parts of yourself that you have come to miss? What effect has those parts of yourself not being there had on your life? Finally, what can you do to start reclaiming those abandoned parts?

_____

_____

_____

_____

_____

_____

_____

_____

_____

_____

_____

Have you begun to see from the very outset how much control you can begin to exercise over your own journey? Hopelessness can give way to a new way of being present in your life—all those things that you dream about but are too frightened to create for yourself. Hopefully you have begun to see how the first steps begin with the choices you make. Simply, do those choices honor who you are or do they appease your little gods?

PART 3

Liberating the Spirit

At the heart of each of us,
whatever our imperfections,
there exists a silent pulse of perfect rhythm,
a complex of wave forms and resonances,
which is absolutely individual and unique
and yet which connects us to
everything in the universe.

-George Leonard

Catching Lightening in a Bottle

Man's main purpose in life is to give birth to himself,
to become what he potentially is.

-Erich Fromm

The last time I said good-bye to her, I felt like a bird nudging her young out of the nest. She was taking three weeks off from her sessions with me to perform in her first play for a school project. The anticipation of this project had dominated our discussions for at least the last month.

We examined every nook-and-cranny—her self-doubts, her fears, all the ways she was shutting down as a result of the stress created by this project. Each week was an exploration of her retreat. Retreat from herself, the people in her life, her responsibilities from life in general.

The symptoms were all the classic signs of a person disconnecting from their spirit. Emotionally numb, feeling depleted of her usual energy, she cut back on her workouts, began to miss work, as well as neglecting her preparation for the play. She found herself in her usual cycle of self-sabotage—feeling blocked, she was lost in her discouraged obsessive thinking, unable to write or plan for her part in the play. Spiritually, to her, this wasn't just another school project, to her this was a life-test, a test she needed to pass in order to validate her life's purpose.

As I said, she had taken three weeks off to devote fully to her project, so I was mighty curious to find out how well things had gone for her. As soon as I saw her, I didn't wonder any more. Her face was aglow, her smile stretched from ear to ear. There was a bounce to her step, a looseness in her body that said it all.

As she walked up to me, I asked, "Well?"

She smiled as she said, "I'll never be the same again."

I gave her my biggest, brightest I-told-you-so smile and said, "You've caught the wave, haven't you? You've discovered that well of energy."

She looked at me and said, "For the first time I finally understand what you mean. These last three weeks, everything just came together. I have never experienced this kind of, well, I don't know the word for it. Harmony? Maybe that's what this feeling is, just like, an engine clicking on all six cylinders.

"I feel like the floodgates opened up all at once. I'm almost afraid of saying this out loud but, I feel like a brilliant light was lit within me. I close my eyes now when I feel confused or momentarily stuck and my mind expands, I don't really know how to explain this, but it expands into a glowing presence."

I nodded as she paused, understanding exactly what she was talking about. "As you were talking, I had a picture in my mind of a lighthouse. It had this strong beacon of light cutting a path through the darkness."

"I'm so afraid of losing this."

"Don't be," I assured her. "Once you've gotten to this point, you'll continue to ride the wave. I can show you how to regain it the times you momentarily disconnect from it."

I never cease to be amazed when I see it happen to somebody for the first time. The transformation is always so dramatic. The transformation in their thoughts, their emotions, in their self-concept, in their physical being, it's all so profound to me. Quite simply, it's the inevitable outcome of what begins to unfold once we make a conscious choice.

Consciously choosing to step out of the shadows is

part of our evolutionary task, it's our deepest existential stirring. As we've already discussed, we start that process by awakening our soul. Once we awaken our soul, the next stage to stepping out of the shadows is unleashing the life-force that enables us to express who we are, express our essence from the depths of our soul. I think of this next step as *Liberating the Spirit*.

Liberating the Spirit. You see a pattern developing? First we awaken, next we set free. But set free what? Well, in its rawest form, we are setting free energy. That's what it's all about. It's energy. It's all about energy.

Spirit? Energy? Life-Force? These are the words I use to think about the quality that fuels my journey. Although these words may take on some sort of mystical aura, there's really nothing mystical about them.

Does the word *convergence* help? It's a coming together of sorts, this life-force thing. Think of our spirit as an endpoint, the endpoint of several different sources of energy coming together. Converging energy, unifying into a whole.

Just what is all of this converging energy? Just what is this elemental energy? It's the sum total of our emotional, behavioral, cognitive, physiological, creative, and spiritual processes. All of these processes converge at one point—unifying, creating a well of energy, a well of energy I think of as our spirit.

You know that saying about the whole being greater than the sum of the parts? Well, when you add together all of our life processes, you wind up with this thing, this quality, this unified whole, very simply a life-force—our spirit.

But let's stick to the game plan. This is where you have

to step in and figure out what *Liberating the Spirit* means to you. Take some time and start formulating for yourself what it means to liberate your spirit.

_____

_____

_____

_____

_____

_____

_____

_____

_____

_____

_____

_____

_____

_____

_____

_____

_____

_____

_____

_____

_____

_____

_____

_____

_____

_____

We need to liberate our spirit as a means of fueling our awakening. We need to free our spirit when it becomes buried under all the ca-ca that we collect throughout our journey.

Do you recognize what it's like in those times when we disconnect from our spirit, become estranged from the power that fuels our life's journey? I certainly see the manifestation of what that looks like in my private practice.

A negativity pervades all we think about ourselves. We question our worth, our value to ourselves or anybody else for that matter. We focus on what we believe our defects are. More and more of our time is spent alone, reinforcing the myth that we are undesirable, even worthless, in the eyes of the world. Disconnected from our spirit, we hold the belief that we lack the fundamental attributes we consider essential to attain happiness and fulfillment.

Does any of this ring true for you? Do you recognize how the way you think and feel towards yourself is affected by the times you're disconnected from your spirit? Take a moment and write about what that experience is like for you.

_____

_____

_____

_____

_____

_____

_____

_____

Are you aware of how the way you think and feel about yourself appears in your life when you are disconnected from your spirit? For example, do you find yourself withdrawing or isolating? Do you find yourself feeling irritable? Do you find yourself giving up on yourself or projects you're involved with? Does apathy erase any vestige of interest you have for participating in life? Take a moment and write about the ways being disconnected from your spirit appears in your life.

_____

_____

_____

_____

_____

_____

_____

_____

_____

_____

_____

_____

_____

Being disconnected from our spirit affects how we view the people and the circumstances in our lives. We tend to see the world as an overwhelming place to live. A place where there's nothing but unreasonable demands being made upon ourselves. We may have a feeling of deprivation. It's as if the world has decided to withhold all that we want and need from the people in our life. Anger begins to consume us as we begin to hold the world responsible for the fact that we feel so lost, so alienated, so disconnected.

When we aren't consumed by our anger at life, we're feeling small and frightened. Small because everything seems to be stacked against us. Frightened because we feel so inadequate; it feels utterly futile, this idea that we can do anything about our life.

When we're disconnected from our spirit, we feel like there's nothing we can do to influence our lives in a positive manner. Losing the sense that we can in anyway positively influence our life, we begin to feel totally out of control.

Once we feel like our life is out of control, we begin to feel a pervasive sense of vulnerability. Now angry at the world, feeling inadequate and powerless to do anything about how our life has drifted, our increasing sense of vulnerability fuels an ever-increasing feeling of hopelessness.

But that spiral of hopelessness and despair does'nt have to remain forever.

"I don't know what it was. Perhaps I was sick and tired of being sick and tired. Maybe the pain of staying the way I was began to exceed whatever pain inevitably comes with change. I wasn't ready to say that my ways were wrong, but I knew that my ways weren't working for me anymore."

Billy was telling me about what made a difference for him. Although we had played on the same softball team for years, we had never taken the time before to talk about what he had been going through. But from the outside looking in, it was obvious to the most casual observer that Billy was living his life differently.

He had become more open with people. There was a

lightness to his mood that didn't exist when we met several years before. Previously, when things hadn't gone his way, he would erupt, but now he seemed to take things more in stride. In general, he was more pleasant to be around and to get to know.

Steve, "I don't know how to put it in the terms that you talk about, but I know that I am grateful for what I have in my life today."

"Well, what do you think has changed for you?" I asked.

"The biggest thing I realize now is how little I really know about myself. Would conscious be the right word? I'm more conscious of myself, my actions," he interrupted himself with a chuckle, "My infamous reactions."

There was a look of self-consciousness on his face. "I don't know if I'm making any sense. I thought I would've been the last person in the world to put stock in any of this stuff. But I gotta tell you, understanding me better has made all the difference in the world.

"I used to think that life was one big encounter, you know, like I had to fight for every last piece of turf. But now I feel like I'm learning how to swim with the current rather than against the current."

"How did you learn to do that?" I asked, hoping to pick up a pointer or two myself.

"You know, that's the damnedest thing about all of this. When we play ball, we know if we swing the bat in just the right way, we'll make contact with the ball. But with this stuff, there doesn't seem to be any direct connection that is obvious to me between what I do and the outcome it's going to have."

"You're starting to lose me now. What are you talking

about?" I asked, feeling somewhat puzzled.

"For instance, when I work out, I feel like the harder I work out, the harder I impose my will on my training, the better my results will be.

"But, you know, I feel kind of stupid for saying this, but, I honestly think I've stopped trying to impose my will and things seem to come out the way I want them to, well at least more times than not. I can't explain it. Like I said, I feel like I've learned how to ride with the current of the river rather than go against it."

"Maybe it has to do with that awareness thing you were talking about?"

"Yea, well, your guess is as good as mine. But I do know that I've started paying attention to *all* of myself."

"All of yourself?" I asked.

"You've watched me for four or five years now. It's pretty obvious that I never thought anything through. I never reflected, I never considered the big picture. I just bounced around, you know, always reacting to life. Well, I know I'm different now in that respect. I listen to other people, I listen to myself. I listen to my body, my heart, not just my hardheaded ways. Hell, I even listen to the mental images that come up when I am trying to relax.

"That's what I've learned, just how to listen to myself and put the pieces together."

"That sounds like a lot of work."

"At first I thought so, but you know what is really hard work? Undoing all the stuff I had to undo when I wasn't listening to myself. Digging myself out of every hole I dug for myself because I was so insistent on running life rather than moving along with it."

Frozen in Time

If you bring forth what is within you, what you bring forth will save you. If you do not bring forth what is within you, what you do not bring forth will destroy you.

-The Gospel of St. Thomas: Logion 45

To the uninitiated, you would think that it's a well choreographed dance. I've participated in it hundreds of times, but I swear the dance is merely a symptom of an imprisoned spirit. It goes something like this.

I greet her at the door. She tries to force a smile. Her mouth moves but her eyes remain flat, there's almost an eerie stillness to them.

As I motion for her to have a seat, I notice how stiff her body is as she lowers herself into the seat. While sitting, her left leg crosses over her right leg, seemingly detached from the rest of her body, as it alternates from mindlessly swinging to laying lifelessly upon her knee.

Her hands anxiously grip the sides of the chair, the whiteness in her knuckles belying the calm exterior she's desperately trying to portray.

As I sit down, my eyes lock onto her eyes for the briefest of seconds and then she looks away from me. Her eyes begin to dart around the room finally coming to rest on a spot in the carpet.

I start the session by asking how she feels about being here.

She looks up, shrugs her shoulders and says, "Oh, I dunno, I feel fine I guess."

Her face is frozen with fear. Her breathing comes in gasps. Her body is stiff as a board. Her eyes appear lifeless. Yet her words, her words report that all is well.

I ask her to tell me a little bit about what she would like to focus our work on.

She talks for awhile about the circumstances with her boyfriend, circumstances that she fines troubling. As she talks, tears begin to well in her eyes, yet she fights them back. Her frozen face becomes etched with the pain that comes from feeling betrayed and abandoned.

I share my observation of how she appears to be hurting. She stares at the ceiling, thinks about it and says, "Naw, I don't think it hurts, I just want to understand what's going on."

She begins to tell me how foolhardy she had been to trust this man. She had changed her life for him. She had let him into her life in ways that she had never done so before. All she got for her trouble was a lot of hard work, eventually having the rug pulled out from underneath her. All the while she's talking, the veins in her neck are protruding, her eyes are the size of quarters—a mixture of hurt, confusion, and rage; her left leg swinging at a furious pace.

I comment on how angry she sounds. She looks at me as if I was talking about a third person in the room. She says, "No, I wouldn't call it anger. I just should have known better."

"What do you mean by that?" I ask her.

"Well, I've made it a point to keep most men at arm's length. I've never really needed to be in a relationship. In fact, I'm much better off without them. Life always seems to go just fine when I stay focused on my work."

I nod at what she is saying. "You're right, not everybody should be in a relationship. But what about your emotional needs. How do your emotional needs get met?"

"I don't know. I don't really think about those things. I just know that I've had to depend on myself my whole life and I've done just fine.

"I don't really think I need anybody else. I get along just fine on my own."

"Does it ever get lonely for you?" I ask.

"You know, I never really thought about it in that way before. It's just the way it's always been."

She then shifts the conversation, telling me about her work, how she's been in her present job for over fifteen years.

"Do you enjoy what you do?"

"It pays the rent."

"Are you good at what you do?"

"I'm alright, I suppose."

"How did you get into this line of work?"

"It's something I just fell into after a couple of other jobs didn't work out."

I remembered her mentioning earlier that she thought of herself as being very aggressive. I found myself wondering what the underside of her aggressiveness was like. I asked her what was at the center of who she was.

"You know, I really don't know," she remarks, dumbstruck by the implications of what she had just revealed to herself.

Every time I have this sort of conversation with somebody, it has the same feel to it. There is a sense of detachment. It's as if we are talking about somebody else's life.

It seems like the person isn't in their body. It's as if they have created an outer shell to engage the world. The essence of whatever it is that defines who they are is missing. Trying to penetrate the shell can be as tricky as trying to cut through a diamond.

The individual is numb, but even more than numb, they are divorced. Divorced from their emotional experience. Divorced from the way their emotions appear in their body, in their conversation, in their day-to-day lives.

I watch. I watch closely. I watch how they go through a

wide range of emotions as they speak, yet, they are totally unaware of that whole process unfolding within themselves.

Their lives appear to be a string of random acts that are not attached to anything that's truly important to who they are. Their life appears to be more a tapestry of random happenstance than any kind of orchestrated process that was in any way connected to the soul of the individual. It's almost as if they're a feather blown by the wind, riding the current of some external force rather than living from within their own soul.

The story that plays in their head is a litany of explanations. Explanations for how they can go *without*, how they don't really *need*, how they get along fine *by themselves*. Always the same theme, the pain of deprivation chosen over the fear and discomfort of participation.

It saddens me to see how the fear they live with creates these stories of denial, denial of their emotions, denial of their very human emotional needs, denial of their pathway to a life of abundance.

To keep the stories going, to lend credence to the stories' validity, they choose a life of emotional impoverishment. Yes, they manage to get along. But at what cost? What does it cost any of us to keep the stories of deprivation and self-sufficiency alive?

I don't think I am being overly dramatic when I say that it's as if their spirit has been imprisoned. Can you see all the ways we disconnect from our spirit? Does the above story stir any glimmer of yourself, the ways in which you are connected and disconnected from your spirit?

You can see the importance of *Liberating the Spirit*, can't you? Do you recognize the following life experiences when the spirit is imprisoned. Does the word *depression* take you anywhere in your own experiences? Does it make sense in any small way that a state of depression is a state of imprisoned energy?

Anxiety. Again, where does the word anxiety take you? Is it possible that anxiety is in some small part energy that needs to be discharged but is stuck within us?

Addiction. Does it stand to reason that addiction is a means of imprisoning our spirit?

Emotional shut down. Can you see how we bottle up our spirit, our life-force when we shut down?

Procrastination. Could this be a means to make time stand still? To keep life from imposing its will upon us? Could it be that we imprison our spirit as a means of avoiding the demands of the here-and-now?

Why the need for all these ways of imprisoning our spirit? Why the need for choking all of the energy out of our lives? Could it be that we mistakenly believe that our best interests are being served somehow by shutting down or withdrawing?

Perhaps at one point in our lives that was the case. Perhaps our very means for self-preservation was served by turning within ourselves, more like escaping inward. But how well does imprisoning our spirit work for us today?

I'm reminded of a story I read in the newspaper recently. There was a man arrested in St. Louis for roaming the streets with a hunting rifle, more specifically an elephant gun, I believe. A policeman walked up to him and asked him why he was carrying this elephant gun around.

The man looked incredulously at the officer and said, "Why, officer, isn't it obvious to you? It's to keep the elephants away from here."

The officer, trying to understand what the man was talking about, took his hat off and scratched his head. His head cocked to the side, his right eyebrow arched, he said to the man, "What are you talking about, there isn't an elephant within five thousand miles of here."

The man, not missing a beat, looked the officer right in the eye and said, "You see, it works!"

Well, self-protection is important to us all. However, many of us devise means to protect ourselves that eventually get us in trouble. But the problem is, oftentimes no one can convince us that many of the ways we protect ourselves aren't necessary, that they don't work, that they really serve to imprison our spirit more than anything else.

Ron and I had a talk once about how unsafe he felt in his world. We discussed the many ways he used to make himself feel protected. What he came to realize over a number of years was that every way he chose to insure his self-preservation also froze his spirit, constricting his world to the point that he was merely living to survive, a prisoner of his means of survival.

"Have you ever felt like you were the only person you could count on, that you just didn't feel safe? Well, that's how it's always been for me. I've felt all alone, unprotected, unable to trust anybody."

"How have you dealt with that, with being afraid all of the time?" I wondered out loud.

"Honestly, I don't think I did, at least I didn't deal with it effectively. I did everything I could to push away my thoughts and my feelings."

"How did you do that?" I asked.

"Oh you name it, I did it. Think about my behavior. You've always kidded me about how rigid I've been.

Always doing things the same way, always staying in a safe but limiting pattern of behavior, day after day. Well, that allowed me to live life on auto-pilot. No surprises. No curve balls. No need to think and feel my way through life. Everything predictable."

"You sound kinda angry about that."

"I am, it's been such a waste. I just can't reconcile the time I've wasted. I feel like I've wasted most of my life.

"And the people. I've known a lot of good people but most of that has gone down the drain. The shame of it is that I set myself up for all of this. Always getting involved with needy partners. Needing people in my life who took and took from me but never gave. All of that, only because I needed them in order to feel important. To feel like I mattered."

"Well, all of that is changing for you, isn't it?" I asked somewhat hopefully.

"Yea, I suppose. Little by little. I've been afraid my whole life. That isn't going to change. But it's hard. It's always been hard for me to experience my life changing or expanding. So the more I try to open my life up, the more anxiety I create for myself."

"Wow, it must feel like you're between a rock and a hard place."

"That's exactly right. Imagine what it's like. For instance, I know the way to make myself safe today is to let people in my life, to allow people to be there for me. However, that can be really hard. It's hard to let go of all of my mistrust, all of my ways of protecting myself. It's hard to let someone's love and affection in. Believe me, I want to and I keep trying, but it's hard for me to trust.

"But little by little I'm finding my way. Little by little

I'm discovering a zest for life, a sense of potency that I never had before."

You can hear the blocked energy in the early part of Ron's story, can you not? Control. Control. Control. That's how Ron has kept it together. That is not to judge Ron, but to understand how fearful he has felt in his world.

Ron's solution was to limit his participation in life: to limit the amount of uncertainty he had to deal with: to limit the stimulation that life had to offer in order to feel safe.

Thankfully, today, Ron is slowly but surely finding ways to open the valve little by little, freeing more and more of his spirit with which to engage life.

Why not stop here and think about your spirit, your life-force. How freely does that life force move through your life? Does it move freely or do you have ways of controlling the flow of the energy?

What are the things that are frightening you to the degree that you need to slow down, or shut down completely, the energy with which you engage the world?

_____

_____

_____

_____

_____

_____

_____

_____

_____

_____

_____

_____

No matter the reason, no matter the means, we can change the story we have created in our head as to why we shut down our energy. We can always find new ways of managing whatever it is that is frightening us. Although disconnecting from our spirit may have seemed like an effective solution for whatever we have been trying to solve up to this point, we all can find ways of liberating our spirit so as to be more present in our lives.

Coming Out of the Dark

Life affords no higher pleasure than that of surmounting difficulties, passing from one step of success to another, forming new wishes, and seeing them gratified. He that labors in any great or laudable undertaking has his [fitigues] first supported by hope, and afterwards rewarded by joy.

-Samuel Johnson

Pathfinder's Tip

*Liberating our spirit requires us to move forward with
courage rather than retreat in fear.*

"Your spirit, um, your spirit, you need to think of it
just like a muscle. You know what I mean, use it or lose
it. If you don't exercise it, your spirit will shrivel up and
die on you."

Jay was giving me his take on *Liberating the Spirit*.

"For me, spirit is not something I need to acquire, I
merely need to exercise it in order to keep it strong."

"Just what do you mean by exercising your spirit?" I
asked Jay.

"The way I think about it, we all come into this world
with a spirit, vibrant, full of energy, ready to take us to
wherever we need to go.

"So none of us are coming from a place of having to
get a spirit. But our world is full of toxic influences that
eat away at our spirit, eat away at..."

"Toxic influences? Just what do you mean by that?" I
interrupted.

"Well, it could be just about anything. The culture
we live in that prizes *doing* above *being*. It could be
neglectful parenting that distorts our early develop-
mental experiences. Our own fears which bend and
twist us in ways that our lives become separated from
our soul, disconnected from our spirit."

"So your point is that our work is to keep strong what

the world around us can inevitably undermine?"

"Exactly! We all need to strengthen our day-to-day presence through the care and nurturance of our spirit. The way to do that is to exercise our spirit, not withdraw from it."

Jay makes an important point. How many of us confuse withdrawing with self-protection? Doesn't it stand to reason that we need to become battle-tested in order for our spirit to remain strong?

Think about the beautiful things in this world that are created out of struggle, out of some pressure being applied. A diamond is created from a lump of coal that's bombarded with intense pressure for thousands of years. Or the beautiful mountain chains in the world: how have they come to be? What about steel? It's bent and shaped into wondrous strength and form.

So too is our spirit. Our spirit is forged and strengthened out of our encounters with adversity, not our avoidance of adversity. You see, adversity forces us to exercise our spirit by using our internal resources. That's what's wonderful about exercising our spirit. The resources for encountering new and challenging situations are within us. Vision. Determination. Creativity. Courage. Hope. Encouragement.

When we watch athletes perform above their usual level, we are in awe of how they reach deep down within themselves to give a record breaking performance. When we are confronted with a new challenge, we all have the same ability to respond. And by doing so, we are exercising our spirit. The more we exercise our spirit, the more confidence and well-being we will bring to other challenges we face in our lives.

If we develop the habit of meeting our challenges head

on rather than retreat, it's likely that we'll emerge from those challenges stronger and wiser. That makes sense doesn't it? Being battle-tested is the means by which we keep our spirit sharp and present. In fact, the act of constantly applying ourselves to experiences that make us dig within ourselves plants seeds that enable our spirit to grow and thereby strengthen itself.

I use a simple visualization when I am confronted with a challenge. I close my eyes and create an image in my mind. It's an image of a forest. And when I picture this forest, I picture a tiny tree hemmed in, forced to grow through the crowded forest toward the light. To make room for itself in the forest, this tree must marshal all of its strength, all of its abilities, all of its resources to grow amid the larger trees. As the tiny tree must use all of its resources in order to survive, so must we use all of our resources in order for our spirits to be liberated and to thrive.

The power of this exercise cannot be underestimated. Can you see how we are all trying to grow towards the light? And it's inevitable that many challenges will lie in our path.

However, it's from these obstacles that we can harvest the resources necessary to complete our journey, rather than use those challenges as excuses not to complete the journey.

So you may be wondering how best to exercise your spirit. Here are but a few ways to get you started.

Freedom Step

Stagnation of the spirit is relieved by action.

Somewhere deep inside of us lie the shackles that imprison our spirit. We have different names for these shackles. What name do you use for your own? Procrastination? Hesitation? Caution? Deliberation? Inertia?

If we find ourselves stuck and feeling frustrated, we need only apply the key that will unlock the shackles that have kept us imprisoned. The key to unlock our personal shackles? Action! Getting started. A mentor of mine once told me, "You can't steal third base if your foot is still on second base."

We can't begin to utilize the power of our spirit if we don't get started. But once we get started, our spirit takes over, pushing us along, almost unconsciously. It's easy to see how the mere act of starting breaks the spell that our stagnant inertia casts upon our lives. Once that spell is broken something very important appears in our life—a sense of control.

With any new stimulation we generate, we feel like we have regained more of our personal power. Personal power that comes out of taking control back from forces that live outside of us. There's nothing more energizing than regaining control of our lives by tapping into the essence of who we are rather than feeling victimized by other people and circumstances.

Picture that in your mind for a moment. A life free of all the negative energy that weighs us down. The inertia of paralysis turned around by the power of spirit.

Can you see how the act of liberating our spirit will compel us to act, to move forward? Picture a jack hammer, breaking up a slab of concrete. Picture how your spirit is as powerful as any jackhammer. Just imagine the concrete that has enslaved your spirit being broken up.

What would the next step be once you felt a little more free? What would you do? Where would you go? Who would you be with? Stepping out of the shadows is an active process. Think of what you want your life to be in terms of action. Don't fall into the trap of merely thinking your way through life.

Action is given birth through our ability to conceive what we want. We have to be able to visualize our outcome. Next we have to visualize the steps necessary to give life to our vision. Quite simply vision plus action equals movement and growth.

Whenever you feel stuck, whenever you feel like you're stagnating, rely on the simple formula I just described. Create a small vision. Make a plan of action. And then go for it. Take it in small steps, but don't let fear turn you back.

Taking action. It's a remedy that's as old as time itself. You know the old saw, "The longest march starts with a first step."

Freedom Step

Invite experiences of growth into our life.

The point of liberating our spirit is that all aspects of our existence, our body, mind, spirit, and soul need to be exercised. No matter our age, no matter our accomplishments, we must continue to invite experiences of growth into our life. It is through these new experiences that we keep our spirit strong.

Growth only takes place when we are challenged. If we want our muscles to grow, what must we do? We must provide resistance. If we want our mind to sharpen we need to feed it new experiences that challenge it to expand.

The same holds true for our spirit. Our spirit needs the stimulation of new challenges in order to prevent atrophy from setting in.

Think for a moment. What are the things that you've been promising yourself you'd do, that you keep putting off? Take a class? Send out your resume? Ask somebody out on a date? Start a project around the house? Start going back to the health club? Learn how to play a musical instrument?

Can you see how doing at least one of those things on your list is a means of exercising your spirit? Can you see how being able to exercise your spirit in this one new way will move you one step closer? That's what it's all about.

Doing things in your life that bring you closer to expressing all of who you are.

You see what I am suggesting here? Stretch. Reach. Go beyond. Create. Out with the old and in with the new. Its value is clear: rejuvenation.

Just what are those things that you let get in your way? What are the obstacles that inhibit your willingness to let new experiences into your life? Why do you choose to give so much power to obstacles rather than your desire to [re]connect?

Now is the time to make small changes. Don't take on anything bigger than you can handle. But I promise you, those small changes are like money in your savings account, they compound interest quarterly. Go for a walk. Maybe you'll make friends with somebody. That new experience may be the impetus that leads to a new place to live, a new hobby to get involved with, a new organization to join. Let's be clear, if you keep on doing what you've always been doing, you're only going to get more of the same.

Exercise your spirit. New experiences are the means by which you feed and nurture your spirit. Strengthening our spirit creates resiliency for ourselves and the obstacles we encounter along the way. New experiences are the means by which we grow towards the light that lies on the horizon.

Freedom Step

Dedicate our life's journey to joy!

[Re]connecting to our life's journey is not a practice of drudgery. Although the work is hard, we all need to make it a labor of love. The aim of our hard work is one thing and one thing only. To lighten our load, to make significant connections with the people in our lives, to share our pain and sorrow with those who can be there for us, and ultimately to transform our life into a celebration.

The simple need for creating joy in our life? It renews us. Joy purifies us, ultimately leaving us with a profound sense of well-being.

Liberating our spirits is the action step that unleashes the whole range of the human experience within ourselves. We have chosen to open ourselves to what it means to be human. We have opened ourselves to express the wonder of what it is to be on Earth. Ultimately it's within our own power to create a life that is full of joy and wonder or experienced as one of drudgery and pain.

The formula is quite simple. Liberating the spirit requires action. Passive introspection just ain't gonna get it. We must rise above the mere act of intellectually trying to free ourselves. Don't settle for mere introspection. Understanding without applying new understandings to our lives renders those new insights impotent.

Secondly, we need to focus on a specific type of action. The action should be one that invites growth into our life. New things that challenge us to stretch ourselves. New things that challenge us to develop differnt ways of thinking, acting, and feeling. New things that challenge us to integrate new aspects of ourselves with the old is the means by which we shed old skin as we grow new skin to live in.

Lastly, the path of transformation can be a lot of hard work. A joyful attitude that invites play into your life is the only antidote I know to the inevitable discouragement and heartbreak that goes with the hard work of [re]connecting to your life's journey.

I am going to stop at this point. The reason is very simple. I want you to build into your own life steps that will liberate your spirit. What I have discussed is a good start only. Please, for your sake, give them a try, but more importantly, create your own program based upon what we have started here.

One Part Courage, Two Parts Faith

As soon as you trust yourself,
you will know how to live.

- Goethe

Pathfinder's Tip

Liberating our spirits requires that we develop faith in
ourselves and the virtue of our journey.

Liberating our spirit is nothing more than the art of cultivating faith. You see for us to step out of the shadows, what is ultimately required of us all is trust and faith, not merely understanding and reason.

Faith in the virtue of our journey? Voltaire said it best, "Faith consists in believing when it is beyond the power of reason to believe."

A chance meeting with Alan at an airport in Denver demonstrates what Voltaire meant. Our plane was delayed by snow so we had lots of time on our hands. We were talking about our careers and the crooked path that we'd taken to get us to the point we were at today.

Alan shared with me a little bit about his story. "I feel like I've lived two lives. My first life, I had no direction, no sense of where I was headed. My decisions weren't decisions as much as they were reactions to events. There was no rhyme or reason to anything that I was doing.

"I had three jobs in seven years, all three in different industries. I was in and out of school, never able to stick to anything I started.

"Relationships were a joke to me. My relationships could have been featured in any self-help book as a prime example of whatever the wrong way to be in a relationship was."

"Whoa, that all sounds rather dramatic, don't you think?" I blurted out.

"Dramatic? Sure, but all true. In fact, I consider myself to be the king of drama.

"But ten years ago, I finally figured some important things out for myself. I forced myself to honestly assess my talents, my twisted value system, and the direction of my life. I started to think about what the important things were in life."

"And?"

"Well, first thing I did was get a divorce. I no longer needed to be wrapped up in all of the ugliness that my marriage held for both me and my wife.

"A few months after my divorce was finalized, I quit my job."

"You quit your job right after you got a divorce!" I exclaimed, not quite knowing whether to admire his courage or question his sanity.

"I figured it was now or never. I knew what I wanted to do. I knew I would have to go back to school and I knew I had a narrow window of opportunity to get it all done."

"And you lived to tell about it," I observed, not able to really comprehend the enormity of what my new friend must have really gone through.

"I'm giving you the *Reader's Digest* version of what changed things around for me, but believe me, it has been an incredibly difficult time.

"Do you know how lonely it gets? The people I thought I could count on for support and encourage-ment, I swear they were doing everything they could to undermine me. Everyone said I was just being paranoid, but the people who I thought would be there for me, I swear, I think they were more threatened than happy for me by what I was doing with my life."

"What got you through it all?" I asked.

"One thing and one thing only—faith. Faith in my vision. Faith in the outcome. Faith in the means I chose to get me there. Faith that the universe would supply me with whatever I was lacking in order to accomplish the transformation I had set out on.

"I had spent the first part of my life giving all of my power to my parents, my teachers, my boss, my wife. I never took responsibility for much of anything.

"When I started assessing everything, I came to the decisions I came to and promised myself one thing. No matter how discouraging the day or even the moment was, I promised myself that I would not run."

"Yea but, come on, we all make those kinds of promises to ourselves, and the moment we get scared, the moment we get the least bit discouraged, boom, we go right back to where we started," I injected somewhat cynically.

"Oh, don't get me wrong, you're absolutely right about that. I had plenty of those moments: no, there's nothing different about me, I'm in no way bulletproof from the ravages of fear and discouragement."

"So what got you through it?" I asked, wanting to know the secrets that Alan obviously possessed.

"It's simple, that is, it's a simple solution, but not so simple to stay with. But I believed in the absolute sanctity of what I started out on. I believed that these decisions were made with a higher purpose in mind than my momentary comfort level. All I needed to do was honor the decisions I made by being true to the course I had set sail on."

"Alan, you're saying that just because you believed in your choices, you were able to see it through?"

"You got it only partially right. I believed in my choices, yes. But for me, I wasn't the architect of these choices, I was merely the general contractor. That meant it was my responsibility to sustain my faith in the outcome of the project, to sustain my faith in those times when I couldn't see what was around the next corner.

"The way I saw it, I wasn't calling the shots any more, I had given that job away. Therefore I had one job and one job only, to keep the flame alive. And believe me, when you make life that simple, when you turn over control of the ship, keeping the flame alive through good times and bad is a cinch."

Alan had given me something to think about. How much faith did I have in myself, my journey, in the wisdom of the universe and its ability to provide the missing pieces? How much certitude did I demand in my life before I would take a step into the land of the unknown? How could I tap into the innate courage that we all possess to connect with our spirit and trust it enough to let it take me wherever it was going to take me?

Well, I was struck by Alan's use of the words *general contractor* and *architect*. I thought maybe I'd have to rearrange my place in the universe. Maybe it was time to quit trying to force my will upon the world. Maybe it was time to admit that I really wasn't doing such a good job as the architect. What my conversation with Alan reminded me of was an old saying a good friend of mine once told me, "Man plans, God laughs." No I decided that it was time for me to get with the universe's program and put my energies into maintaining my faith in that.

So I wrote a letter to myself. It has served as a compass, a guide for my life, if you will. Sure, I stray, get lost, become disoriented but this is what I consult first when I feel lost and off course. I carry the original in my wallet to this very day. Although it's torn and tattered, it's one of my most precious possessions.

Steve:

No matter what life lays in your path, believe in yourself and the sacredness of your journey. Don't give that up for anybody or anything. No one can live in your place. No one can understand the push and pull of your life and the choices you make.

Don't let fear dominate your life. Put it in its proper place. To be oblivious to it, is to be imprisoned by bars you cannot see. To make it your god, is to be enslaved by an influence that is toxic. Let fear teach you what it can about who you are, what lives inside of you, how you can use what is inside of you to grow beyond these temporary obstacles.

Faith is the strongest weapon you can use against the ups and downs of life. Your faith can only evolve out of a singular belief. A belief in a power that is beyond the realm of knowing, seeing, touching, tasting, hearing, or smelling. Fusing your spirit to the strength of that power will enable you to be a serious player in this game of life.

Don't lose sight of the obvious. To abandon the gift of faith is to abandon yourself. To ignore the gift of faith is to diminish a part of who you are. To oppose the gift of faith is to destroy a part of who you are. To align with the gift of faith is to liberate yourself and experience true indepen-

dence. It is this very state of being that can be true liberation for you.

I refer to this letter as my *Letter of Liberation*. It provides me with a wonderful gift: *perspective*. Whenever I become myopic, whenever I lose sight of the big picture, I pull this letter out. It literally frees me from the tentacles with which the fear of the unknown entangles my life. We all get hooked from time to time. That's a given. But any tool we can use to get us unhooked is a gift.

How about you? How do you get unentangled? Why not take some time and try to write your own *Letter of Liberation*?

_____

_____

_____

_____

_____

_____

_____

_____

_____

_____

_____

_____

_____

_____

_____

_____

_____

_____

Give this letter the time and attention that it deserves, even if you only work on it five minutes at a time. This letter can be the beginning of an important but subtle shift in how you live your life. Just keep this in mind as you wrestle with composing the letter. The process of writing the letter can be very uplifting, being true to the spirit of the letter is an act of emancipation.

PART 4

Illuminating the Path

No one can persuade another to change.
Each of us guards a gate of change that can only be
opened from the inside.

-Marilyn Ferguson

Developing 20-20 Vision

Your vision will become clear
only when you can look inside your own heart.
Who looks outside, dreams;
who looks inside, awakes.

-Carl Jung

The next step is brutally simple, yet undoubtedly one of the more frightening steps to apply. For after we awaken to what we want our lives to be, after we awaken to how we have drifted from what that picture looks like for us, after we have liberated the energy that lifts us out of our paralysis, we need to set out in a new direction.

Although a new direction may be what we desire most in our lives, discovering the direction that will honor the awakening that we have undergone can still be an elusive end to achieve. For not only do we need to discover a path that is uniquely suited to who we are, we also need to learn how to pass on the inevitable temptations of following a path that is the creation of someone other than ourselves. I refer to the next step as *Illuminating the Path*. I can best explain it in the following story I once heard.

It's a story about a man who had set out on a very special journey, a search if you will. This man was determined to discover the one true path that would bring him to his own spiritual awakening. You see, he had studied the various spiritual ways of the world, never really settling on any one path to follow. So he set out to find someone who could prescribe for him the one true path that would best serve the awakening he so desperately wanted to experience.

For ten years, he went from spiritual leader to spiritual leader trying to get each and everyone of them to tell him what the one true way was. But time after time, he had the same experience.

He would follow their way for awhile, become

dissatisfied and leave. He roamed the world, going from spiritual leader to spiritual leader, following their way but never being satisfied with their practices or what their practices brought him.

After ten years of searching, his travels brought him to the foot of the tallest mountain in all of India. There he was informed that if he climbed the mountain to the very top he would discover the answer he had been searching for.

Our searcher, ever the adventurer, set out on foot to climb the mountain. After three weeks of brutal physical exertion, the man came to the last ledge that he had to climb in order to complete his daunting ascent.

As he boosted himself up over his final hurdle, there before his very eyes his long sought after answer appeared. For as he reached the top of the mountain, he stood before a pool of water from which he saw his own reflection shimmering against the bright light of the noon sun. And all at once the answer came rushing into his consciousness, the answer that he had been seeking from everyone with whom he had spoken over the last ten years. The answer, simple but profound, "My true path lives only within myself."

Upon hearing that story for the first time, I realized how I too was looking everywhere but within myself for the one path that would honor my life. You know that song *Looking for Love in All the Wrong Places*? Well, I promised myself that I would stop looking to others for the answers that lived only within me.

As a result of that pledge to myself, I have created over the years a set of criteria to follow that keeps my path illuminated, allowing me to determine where I am, whether I have strayed, or how true I am being to my path.

When I think of others before myself, my path is illuminated.

When I maintain a discipline that nourishes my mind, body, spirit, and soul, my path is illuminated.

When I act spontaneously, my path is illuminated.

When my actions are a reflection of my life's purpose, my path is illuminated.

When I rise above my fears to do what I must do next, my path is illuminated.

When I take responsibility for my emotional and spiritual well-being, my path is illuminated.

When I am flexible enough to withstand the never-ending winds of change, my path is illuminated.

When I steel myself by remaining grounded by my life's vision, my path is illuminated.

When I allow myself to adapt to the circumstances of my life rather than forcing the circumstances to conform to my life's plan, my path is illuminated.

When I offer forgiveness to myself rather than condemnation and shame, my path is illuminated.

Although I have devised my own means by which I light my path, there is nothing simple about keeping the lights from flickering out. No indeed, in the course of learning how to illuminate the path of my life's journey, I have discovered that there are basic elements that keep the flame alive.

The first elements that I am referring to? In a word, *trust*. Learning to trust ourselves. Trusting ourselves that we know what is best for us. How many of us have gone through life not trusting ourselves? Not trusting what we think. Not trusting what we feel. Not trusting the choices we make.

Roland understands how important trusting himself is. For much of his life he focused on others rather than centering himself from within.

"I grew up in my family always feeling like I was crazy. When I tried to tell someone what I was feeling, my feelings were minimized or belittled. 'Oh, you're too sensitive, you're always overreacting' was the way I was always dismissed. When I tried to tell someone what I was experiencing, I was told to shut up. When I tried to tell someone what I thought, my thoughts were questioned.

"So I learned to ignore my experiences, I learned to invalidate what I was thinking and feeling. Most damaging of all, I learned how to look to others to affirm what I was experiencing about myself and the people in my life.

"The result was that I never pursued what I wanted, because I could easily talk myself out of it. Afterall, why subject myself to the inevitable second guessing, the inescapable belittlement. That only served to make the noise in my head, you know, the self-doubts, even the self-loathing, get louder and louder.

"You know, I had to do a lot of spring cleaning in my life. I couldn't really begin to trust myself until I found people in my life who encouraged me. People who understood what it meant to support me. People who understood that I could learn best by doing for myself rather than being told what to do. People who knew how to let me pick up the pieces when I fell, rather than wag their finger at me and say 'I told you so.'

"Their kindness and respect acted as a mirror, teaching me how to trust myself as they invested their trust and faith in me."

A second element of keeping the flame alive is

fortitude. The internal strength we all possess to withstand the discouragement of setbacks and wrong turns. The strength that we all possess to calm ourselves in times of crisis. Being able to withstand the tides of doubt. The doubt washing over us, tugging at us, tripping us up, making us dive for cover with each new step we take. The doubt foisted upon ourselves by others who would rather pull us down because of their own fear, their fear of losing us if we heal, grow, and transform. The doubt that lives within ourselves, the self-doubt so easily activated whenever we feel like we are venturing out on our own.

Whenever I am feeling unnerved, whenever doubt creeps into my life, whenever fear overtakes me, causing me to second guess myself, I have a very simple exercise I do. I turn the world off for fifteen minutes. I simply sit in a chair, close my eyes, and focus on my breathing. That's all there is to it. But you would be amazed at how restorative that simple little exercise can be.

The final element I rely upon to keep the flame burning bright? In a word, *patience.* If we follow a path that flows from within ourselves, then we will experience our lives as a series of trials. Quite simply, life is full of pain and suffering. We will be tested by the trials that appear along the way. The choice will always be there for us: persevere or turn around.

What we learn from our journey is that there is nothing in life that does not extract some cost. More importantly, there is nothing in life that can be achieved without going through a series of small trials.

Herb knows the value of patience. He has learned the hard way about the game of life, the fact that you don't hit a home run with one swing of the bat. Herb was in drug rehab five times before that truism sunk in for him.

"For me, it was always easier to give up, give in. I would always choose self-indulgence over patience. I knew the steps I was suppose to take whenever I wanted to use. Call my sponsor. Get to a meeting. Call somebody from my contact list. I could have taken a quiet time or read the *Big Book*.

"I didn't get it, you know, I didn't get that being sober meant more than just not drinking. It meant doing every little step along the way that went into not drinking.

"I didn't understand one very important fact. Sobriety was a state of being, a way of life, not an act of abstinence. I had to learn that not drinking was the outcome of continual striving, patiently doing all of the little things. Once I figured that out, I was able to stop indulging every little whim I had."

How about ending things up for this section by doing our familiar exercise. What about this step *Illuminating the Path*? For me, the path is turning inward for our answers. Cultivating a level of awareness that will enable us to transcend the limits that we experience by following our own conscious thoughts over the directives of others. Discovering the essence of our path—patience, perseverance, and our own inner strength.

But how about for you? Where does this idea of a path take you? What does it mean to you to *Illuminate the Path*? More importantly what is the means by which you want to light that path? Take your time with this one.

It's critical for you to devise for yourself a path that is meaningful for you and you only. We are trying to find the vessel by which you can express the energy that is beginning to stir deep within you. Let yourself be as creative as you dare to be. For it is this very creativity that will help you shape your life's journey into the way that does you the most honor.

_____

_____

_____

_____

_____

_____

_____

_____

_____

_____

_____

_____

_____

_____

_____

_____

_____

_____

_____

_____

_____

_____

_____

_____

_____

_____

_____

This is where the fun starts, yet at the same time there is an enormous burden in taking total responsibility for our well-being. What we can expect is that both fear and exhilaration will wash over us quite often. That's the wonder of what lies ahead for us all. New experiences, new territories to be explored, new adventures to live out, and most of all, life lived in the lightness of the here-and-now rather than the darkness of all the tomorrows that never come to fruition.

The biggest thrill of all? We get to start *navigating* this journey!

Which Way to Albuquerque?

*The great thing in this world
is not so much where we are,
but in what direction we are moving.*

-Oliver Wendell Holmes

Pathfinder's Tip

*Our path is illuminated when we focus on becoming
more of who we are rather than continually trying
to become who we are not.*

There's no getting past this tip. Yet sadly, we all can
look back on parts of our life where we have invested our
emotions, our time, and our money trying desperately to
escape the inescapable. We are who we are. To pursue a
path that promises to transform us into what we are not
is sheer folly.

In fact, the more we violate this principle, the more we
try to stop ourselves from being who we are, the more we
wind up super-charging our life's energy with the very
characteristics we do not want.

I see this all the time in my Relationship Bridge
Building groups. Alvin is a good example of how this
happens. Alvin desperately wants to be viewed as kind,
earnest, sincere, well intentioned. He's quite wary of
upsetting anybody, not wanting to risk being disliked. He
hides how angry he is, how judgmental he is about most
of the people in the group. To each group member's face,
he tells them how much he cares for them, but his
behavior appears to be anything but caring. He's often
withdrawn, emotionally unavailable. Alvin is quick to
offer a word of kindness when he is challenged to
participate more, to give more of himself.

However, the group members are never satisfied with his words. He is often experienced by the group members as patronizing, insincere, withdrawn, and unavailable. And this confounds Alvin to no end. Afterall, doesn't he always say the right thing, doesn't he always do the right thing, doesn't he always hide how angry and judgmental he can be?

But seemingly to no avail. The lesson Alvin needs to learn is both simple and frightening at the same time. Become more of who you are rather than creating someone who you are not.

Easy to say but how do we exercise it? Focus on two things: attitude and action.

The attitude? Accept where you are. Accept the simple fact that we are growing; afterall, our journey is a process of transformation. We are where we are in our lives today, but that doesn't have to stay that way forever. It's always tempting to compare ourselves to others, defining ourselves solely by what we are not because we focus on what we believe others to be. Unfortunately, this is a formula for pain, a formula for chasing an ever elusive way of being.

Ralph knows the shame he brings to himself every time he belittles himself for lacking what he believes others have but he is so sorely lacking. He focuses on the fact that he isn't kind enough, patient enough, forgiving enough, smart enough, slim enough, perky enough. *Enough. Enough. Enough.* Ralph seldom thinks about what he is, because he is always focused on what he is not *enough of.*

Ralph has limited his job opportunities, the opportunities to be in loving relationships, he has even passed up opportunities to live in exotic places where he would much rather live. The reason why? He never believed he was *enough*. But Ralph is slowly learning that he can accept where he is at today, that this acceptance does not condemn him to remain that way forever.

Ralph has learned to trust that he will grow in his own time and his own way without the need to condemn himself for what he is not. If you asked Ralph, he would tell you that it isn't easy, this idea of accepting where he is at, but he also realizes that the universe will provide him with the opportunities he needs to grow, and those are really the only worthwhile lessons to experience.

The action? Let go of the judgments we hold against ourselves. There is nothing that pushes us further away from who we are than the judgments we hold against ourselves. We recognize all those things about who and what we are that we judge, that we dislike. Is *despise* too strong a word? We recognize all the ways we have of covering up, glossing over, disconnecting as a means of honoring those judgments.

Letting go of our judgments is the path to stepping out of the shadows. It's the means by which we accept where we are in our life's journey. It's the path we all walk in order to claim who we are rather than deride ourselves for what we are not.

That's a hard lesson to absorb. For we all want personal growth. We all long for the freedom that comes along with a better understanding of how to better live life. In order to enjoy such freedom we only need to liberate ourselves from a myth that binds us. We cannot *will* ourselves to a different life. We cannot push our way to a different life.

There's only one lesson for us to embrace. Don't judge yourself for not being anything more than who you already are. The energy you invest in who you are today will forge the path for who you are to become in the tomorrows of your life.

Let's Play the Match Game

*We are the products of editing,
rather than authorship.*

-George Wald

Pathfinder's Tip

Our path is illuminated when the essence of who we are is expressed in the way we live our life.

People often ask me if my life has changed much since my first two books, *Building Better Bridges* and *Moving Mountains*, were published. I tell them that nothing has changed except for one thing.

You see, there's one person in my life who has made it her personal mission to see that nothing about me changes. She keeps me grounded. She reminds me of who I am. She spares no words when she thinks I am getting too big for my britches.

I wrote about her in *Moving Mountains*. Her name is Sylvia. She's been tending bar for almost forty years. For the last fifteen years my name, in her mind, was simply *Little Stevie*. But that is the one thing that has changed since I have started writing.

I am no longer *Little Stevie*. No, whenever I go visit her now, upon seeing me she immediately yells out, "Well, if it isn't Mr. Big-Shot-Writer" or "So Mr. Big-Shot-Writer, what'll it be?"

Well, a couple of weeks ago I went to visit Sylvia. I was on a mission of sorts. I had just finished a meeting with my editor, showing her the outline for this book. My editor was mystified that I had left Sylvia out of this book, so I was instructed to go see Sylvia and get her to make some kind of contribution.

I reluctantly agreed to go. You see Sylvia has been getting harder to live with since her appearance in *Moving Mountains*.

So I walked into the bar and there was Sylvia with the ever-present cigarette hanging out of her mouth, leaning on the top of the bar, gabbing with a couple of the regulars. As soon as she saw me, she motioned for me to join her, pushing two of the customers out of the way so that I could sit at the bar.

"Well, Mr. Big-Shot-Writer, how nice of you to come around to see me, where ya been?" she asked.

I explained to Sylvia how busy I had been, reminding her that I had called her twice in the last week to check up on her.

"So, Mr. Big-Shot-Writer, what brings you around tonight?" Her tone told me she was not at all placated by the idea that I had been keeping in touch.

I explained to Sylvia about the meeting I had with my editor and her request to have Sylvia contribute to the new book I was working on.

Sylvia stared at me for a moment, then smiled. Before I could bat an eye, she quickly reached underneath the bar, pulling out a file that was at least three inches thick.

As she leafed through the file, she said, "You know Mr. Big-Shot-Writer, I've been making some notes, you know, just in case you needed me to help you again with your next book.

"Now I've been thinking about how we can do this book a little differently. You know your last book, *Running On the Hillside?*"

"Uh, that would be *Moving Mountains*," I corrected her.

With that said, in one swift motion, Sylvia grabbed a bar towel and flicked it at my forehead, striking me between the eyes. "I told you to stop correcting me all of the time!"

As I wiped the tears from my stinging eyes, I thought to myself that this is what they must mean when they say an artist must suffer for his craft.

"Anyway, that book—it had way too many words in it. We can make this one a lot shorter."

"We're writing a book, not a brochure," I offered somewhat defensively.

"Yea, yea, you're always so sensitive. Now listen to me. If your readers follow this one idea, they won't need to read anything else."

"Well, tell me what the idea is and I'll see if we can use it," I said somewhat impatiently.

"Now settle down, just settle down and I'll tell you, you hear?" she shot back.

"Are you ready? Now listen real careful."

With that said, she leaned over and whispered in my ear as if she was about to reveal some secret concerning national security. "Your innards gotta match your out-ards," she whispered.

"What?!" I exclaimed, feeling like I was in a time warp talking to ol' Granny Clampett.

"You know what I mean. Your life is working for you when your life on the outside matches the inside of you."

"No, I don't know what you mean," I said, slumping forward in my chair, my head falling to the bar top.

She slugged me in the arm and said, "Well then, listen real good, Mr. Big-Shot. I was with Marge yesterday. We were shopping for some furniture for her new apartment.

Anyway, the man who waited on us, he was a miserable soul. You know how I can tell?"

She didn't wait for me to answer.

"His insides didn't match his outsides. His mouth smiled at us but his eyes were dark as night. He talked real fast but his words didn't say a damn thing. He acted like we were the most important people in the world, but he always kept one eye peeled on the front door checking out whether he was missing out on his next customer."

"So?" I said not getting her point.

"Listen, sonny. I've been behind this bar a long time. I've seen them come and go. Oh, you got your big fancy words for it, depression, anxiety, what's that word you taught me a couple of weeks ago, actual..., actual...?

"Self-actualization," I muttered.

"I don't need any of those big fancy words. You know why? I can tell the happy ones from the not so happy ones. You know how I can tell?"

I had an answer all ready for her but she kept talking without pause.

"The happy ones, they always match. Their eyes, their eyes tell me a story about who they are on the inside. No one can fake the eyes. And that's what I'm trying to tell you. This guy wasn't real. He didn't want to be there selling furniture. He didn't want to be there dealing with us."

"But what is so damn helpful about you and Marge buying furniture from this guy?"

"You tell 'em Mr. Big-Shot-Writer, you tell your readers that Sylvia says to start getting their lives to match."

"Match what?" As usual, I was totally exasperated trying to follow her logic.

"What they're doing with who they are? Listen, life is hard

enough without making it harder, you know what I mean?

"We all need to find our place in life and be happy with whatever that is. We all need to know our insides, so we can get our outsides to match.

"So many people are like zombies. You know how I can tell?"

I started to mouth my answer but she didn't take that as a signal to stop and listen.

"They wind up with jobs that don't match them, they wind up with boyfriends, girlfriends, husbands, wives, all of them, they don't match. They wind up spending most of their lives doing things that don't match what they like to do.

"Do you ever ask 'em why, Mr. Big-Shot-Psychologist? 'Cause I don't get it. Why do so many of them refuse to let go of their lives? You know, let go of all of that dead weight?"

I scratched my head and ticked off the some of the reasons I had been told throughout the years. "I dunno, mortgages to be paid; retirement plans to maintain; don't want to disappoint their parents; don't want to hurt their children; it's a lot more complicated than you make it seem, Steve; it's easier to stay quietly numb; I don't believe I deserve anything different; it's my parents' fault."

"That's what I'm trying to tell you, Mr. Big-Shot. Look at me. I've been tending bar my whole life. Been with my old man forever. Got more hobbies than I have time for. Organize the bake sale for the food shelter every year. I love it all. Know how you can tell?"

I quickly put my hand over her mouth and hurriedly shouted out, "Because it matches!"

As she removed my hand from her mouth she said with a look of satisfaction, "You betcha Mr. Big-Shot-

Writer, because it matches."

Alright, so Sylvia may have a point. In fact, I know she does. *Illuminating the Path*–our inside matching our outside. I suppose that is the eventual outcome of awakening our soul and liberating our spirit.

The word I would use is *congruent*, but that really is the same as *matches*. When people come to see me, they really are searching for what that match is. They may not say it that way. They may not even recognize it that way, but much of the pain we experience in our life stems from the fact that some aspect of our lives doesn't match the essence of who we are.

Time and time again I walk down the very lonely path with another person, helping them discover what is locked up inside them. I often think of it as finding a magical lamp that lives inside of us. You know what I mean? There is this old dusty lamp inside of us that we only need to dust off and release the magical genie that lives within.

Once the genie is released, we only need learn how to use the genie to help us construct a life that is congruent with who we are. Or in the words of Sylvia, "We only need to have our innards match our outards."

PART 5

Transforming the Mindset

*What I see without is a reflection of what I have
first seen within my own mind. I always project into
the world the thoughts, feelings, and attitudes which
preoccupy me. I can see the world differently by
changing my mind about what I want to see.*

-Gerald Jampolsky

Making the Mind Quicker Than the Eye

If you are distressed by anything external,
the pain is not due to the thing itself,
but to your estimate of it;
and this you have the power to revoke at any moment.

-Marcus Aurelius

Robespierre was one of the world's greatest mountain climbers in the early 1900's. The story is often told of the time he was climbing a mountain in his native country. While trying to maneuver around a particularly narrow turn, he kicked loose some stones which caused him to lose his footing. Having lost his footing, he fell over the edge of the mountain plummeting to his sure death.

While tumbling through the air, miraculously he managed to grab hold of the roots of a tree that was attached to the side of the mountain. As he was dangling from the roots, he tried desperately to kick himself back over the side of the mountain to safety.

The more Robespierre tried kicking himself to safety, the more he pulled the roots out from the side of the mountain. As he stared down at the razor sharp rocks at the bottom of the valley below him, he realized that his death was inevitable.

Believing he had no other recourse, Robespierre finally looked to the heavens to enlist the help of his God. He shouted at the top of his lungs, "Lord, please, please help me out of my troubles. I will do anything you ask of me if only you will rescue me!"

Robespierre waited for a signal. Finally he heard the voice of the Lord shouting back down to him. "Of course I will help you my son, just let go."

By now Robespierre was drenched in sweat, his grip loosening because of his sweaty hands. He took in the Lord's words, looked to the bottom, and imagined his life ending on those jagged rocks.

Not trusting the Lord's intentions, he again cried out for help, protesting the wisdom of the Lord's plan. But the Lord again shouted out, "Just let go."

Robespierre again looked down at the jagged rocks at the bottom of the valley, looked over to the side of the mountain and saw the roots all but coming loose, looked upward to the heavens with the Lord's solution ringing in his ears, finally he shouted out to the heavens, "Can I get a second opinion from someone else up there?"

Well, much of our experiences with transforming our lives is the never ending battle between holding on and letting go. One of the things that we cling to hardest and longest is the way in which we think about and see the world.

Just like Robespierre, although we may reach out to others for help, although we may choose to surrender our battle with whatever aspect of our life we are at war with, it never ceases to amaze me how we inevitably reject the solution that is right under our nose if that solution doesn't coincide with what we want the solution to be.

But don't despair. There's a remedy for that. That remedy brings us to the next step. This is the step of empowerment. This step is the means by which we can exert the most influence in any area of our lives.

This step is called *Transforming the Mindset*. For me, transforming our mindset is the key to reclaiming our personal power in any given situation. Our ability to transform our mindset can make friends out of our enemies, replace our fears with seeds of courage, and transform seemingly immovable obstacles in our path into opportunities for growth.

Transforming the Mindset is a step towards

empowerment? Well, think about this for a moment. What is the one thing that robs us of our personal power? Is it our insensitive boss? Is it our uncaring family? Is it a chronic disease? Is it a bad economy that keeps us from doing what we want to do with our lives?

Well, all of those things may be true about our family, friends, and life circumstances. But the bottom line is not what our circumstances are but how we view those circumstances, how we evaluate those circumstances, how we evaluate ourselves in the context of those circumstances. That is really what determines whether or not we feel empowered.

Can you see how that is so? Let me share with you a story that a teacher of mine once told.

It seems that there was an all-star executive in a Fortune 500 company. This man was greatly admired for his ability to turn around failing companies bought by his parent company. Once a month he would report to his CEO the results that he had achieved from the previous month. The only rub to this man's performance was a rather embarrassing problem. You see, whenever he would give his monthly report to the CEO, he would wet his pants.

The man's boss, wanting to help his star employee, suggested that he go see a doctor to have the problem treated.

At the next month's meeting, the CEO was surprised to see that the man still had wet his pants.

The CEO inquired of his employee whether he had gone to see the doctor or not.

The man replied, "No I couldn't make an appointment with the one you suggested, so I went to see a psychologist instead. And guess what, he cured me."

"He cured you," the CEO responded somewhat exasperated. "What do you mean, you are still wetting your pants."

"Oh, I know that sir, but I no longer feel the least bit embarrassed about it."

Although the story has a funny twist to it, it really makes the point that I am trying to convey. We don't have to insist that the circumstances of our life change, we only need to change the meaning we give to the circumstances of our life.

What does it take to change our relationship to the events in our life? We merely need to approach our life with a degree of flexibility for how we view the events that are happening in our lives. Simple to say, hard to do. But think about this.

More years ago than I care to remember, I went to a summer camp. The food was awful. The mosquitoes made a smorgasbord out of every part of my body. We were forced to swim in the coldest water you can imagine. There were so many crickets out at night I could barely get three hours of sleep on any given evening. The stars shined so brightly through my window, that if the crickets didn't keep me night, the light from the stars surely did. Clearly, I was not a happy camper. And I was never shy about letting anybody know it.

But that all changed one day when a very wise camp counselor asked me a question I had no answer for.

He simply said, "Everything here bothers you. The food, the water in the lake, the mosquitoes, the stars, the crickets. All these things are imposing upon your life. Let me ask you one thing. When the crickets chirp away at night, how do you know that the crickets are bothering you? Could it be that your energy is going out and bothering them? Just whose life is imposing upon whose life?"

Well, that was like a splash of cold water in my face. I learned much that day. One, that I am not the only one living on planet earth. Two, what I view as the source of my discomfort is inevitably just someone else's way of expressing who they are. Three, by changing how I view those things I experience as antagonistic to my well-being, I no longer have to feel depleted by those circumstances.

Transforming our mindset is a process of letting go of certain assumptions that we carry about ourselves and our place in the world; letting go of our self-centered egocentricity; letting go of the notion that everything done is done to us and against us. How would our lives be different if we stopped personalizing what is done and said to us?

Let go of the belief that the world must conform to our way of living and being. Accept the notion that other people have as much right to take up space on planet Earth as we do. Furthermore, others are entitled to make their place here in a way that makes sense to them, not as would be most comfortable for us.

By living in a space of acceptance rather than condemnation, we can let go of our feelings of victimization. That is what brings us back to how we can empower ourselves. Transforming our mindset from that of a victim. That requires that we think of ourselves as empowered, we see ourselves as empowered, and we act as if we are empowered. Quite simply victimization means that we are welded to one viewpoint of the world, whereas empowerment implies that we have choices about how we act, think, and feel.

Give this step some serious thought. Is it possible by shifting how you think about yourself and the people in your world, that your life can be enhanced? Is it possible that the *problems* in your life are oftentimes created by your continued insistence to hold onto your viewpoint of the world? Is there any value in learning how to transform the relationship between the events in your life and the way you think about those events?

Use the rest of this section as an opportunity to create your own meaning for *Transforming the Mindset.*

_____

_____

_____

_____

_____

_____

_____

_____

_____

_____

_____

_____

_____

_____

_____

_____

_____

_____

_____

_____

_____

_____

_____
_____
_____
_____
_____
_____
_____
_____
_____
_____
_____
_____
_____
_____
_____
_____
_____
_____
_____
_____
_____

What are the things that your mind clings to with absolute certainty? Does that unshakable belief in those things support your well-being, undermine your well-being, or a little of each? If so, how does it do any of those things?

_____
_____
_____
_____

_____

_____

_____

_____

_____

_____

_____

_____

_____

_____

_____

_____

_____

What are the shifts that you might create about how you view the people and the circumstances in your life that would enhance your emotional and spiritual well-being?

_____

_____

_____

_____

_____

_____

_____

_____

_____

_____

_____

_____
_____
_____
_____
_____
_____
_____
_____
_____
_____
_____
_____
_____
_____
_____
_____
_____

Don't be frightened off by the enormity of what I am purposing here. What I am talking about doesn't start and end within this book. However, we need to get started at some point. Make no mistake about it, it is difficult for any of us to get to where we want by holding onto our current limited mindset.

Stepping out of the shadows requires much give and offers very little take. We can be just like Robespierre, we can hold out for the solution that sounds most pleasing to us, that offers the least amount of pain, but in the end, holding out for what we want will likely do us in.

Shifting from Victim to Survivor

*The girl who can't dance says the band
can't keep time.*

- Yiddish Proverb

Pathfinder's Tip

Taking responsibility for our emotional and spiritual well-being requires that we let go of the past by taking ownership of the here-and-now.

A few years ago, I went to a party with a good friend of mine, Beverly. It was quite cold that evening so Beverly wore her full length fake fur coat.

Now this coat is the biggest, furriest thing that you have ever seen. When we arrived at the party, our host took Beverly's coat and put it in the spare bedroom. As the evening wore on, Beverly came up to me and told me that she was ready to leave. Next, she went upstairs to get her coat out of the spare bedroom.

A few moments later, I heard the loudest, shrillest, shriek I had ever heard. I recognized immediately that it was Beverly who had begun to scream hysterically.

Well, naturally I went running up the steps to see what had happened. There I saw Beverly, her body trembling, her hands glued to the sides of her head, screaming at the top of her lungs.

It wasn't until I was able to help her calm down that I could even understand what she was trying to say.

You see, Beverly was deathly afraid of dogs. She had been her whole life. When she was three years old, while sitting in her stroller one day, she was viciously attacked by a huge dog. She received over one-hundred stitches and was obviously very traumatized by the whole situation.

Well, evidently when Beverly went into the dark bedroom, she saw this huge pile of fur laying on the bed and immediately assumed it was a dog. She became overwhelmed with fear and anxiety and bolted from the room.

I didn't want to upset Beverly any more than she already was, but I was somewhat confused. You see, I knew that the people who had given the party didn't have a dog. So I spent a considerable amount of time trying to assure her that there wasn't a dog in the room.

The funny thing was, the more I tried to convince her that there wasn't a dog in the room, the angrier she got with me. In trying to be helpful, it seemed I was making matters worse.

I finally convinced her to come with me into the room so that I could show her that there was nothing to be frightened about.

She finally agreed. We slowly crept up to the doorway and peaked into the room. Sure enough, there on the bed sat this big furry, lumpy creature. Now I was really puzzled.

I cautiously stepped into the room, fumbling around in the dark, searching for a light switch.

All the while Beverly was peeking over my shoulder, nervously clinging to my back.

Finally, I found the switch. After the light came on, we both began to laugh uncontrollably.

For when the light came on in the room, what do you imagine we saw laying on the bed?

That's right! It wasn't a dog at all. It was Beverly's very own fur coat!

Dogs, fur coats, transforming our mindset? The connection? As I said earlier, transforming our mindset is a giant step towards personal empowerment. Just as Beverly discovered, we can be brought to our knees with fear, not by what we encounter in our life, but by our *perception* of what we encounter. If we want to reclaim our personal power, we need to be able to tell the difference between the *dogs* and the *fur coats* that we meet on our path.

Here's another way to think about that. If the *dog* represents our past and the *fur coat* symbolizes the here-and-now, we need to start to distinguish between what is the here-and-now and what is the past leaking into the here-and-now.

You can see from Beverly's experience that when we become more clear about what we are reacting to—either the present or the past leaking into the present—we can more clearly assess what is happening to us in the moment. The value of this is simple to understand. Our fears don't have to overtake how we react to any situation when we are grounded in the moment, for we are *clean* about what is happening with us in the moment.

We only need to discover how the past colors our perceptions of the present. You can think of how that may be true for you, can't you? Something may be happening to us now, but that circumstance may become supercharged with the past leaking into the moment. Just like Beverly's strong reaction when she thought her coat was a dog.

Once she thought that her coat was a dog, it was all over for her, because the trauma she experienced at the age of three immediately colored how safe she was feeling in the present moment. Once Beverly was able to shed some light on the here-and-now, she was able to see that her *misperception* of the coat was the cause of her fear. Then she was able to laugh it off, feeling silly for her overreaction.

By transforming what we see with our mind's eye, we can *empower* ourselves to live a life in the present that is clean and unencumbered. In order to transform what we see with our mind, we need to learn how to clean the lenses of the past through which we view the world.

Clean the lenses through which we view the world. Does that mean that we have to accept the notion that our way is not the only way to see the world? In a word, yes.

You see, we have one thing that is always intruding on our perception of the present moment. That one thing is our past. Our past colors everything we see. Our past colors the judgments we make about the present. Ultimately, our past colors the way we relate to the people and circumstances we encounter in our present.

We work hard in our Relationship Bridge Building groups to develop the skills necessary to separate the past from the present. What I tell the group members is that we need to clean the mud off our windshields before we can start to have a relationship with people in the here-and-now. Quite simply, we need to learn how to view the circumstances and people in our lives in the here-and-now, aided by the understanding of how our past can distort our perception of the present.

Paradoxically, it is often this very tenet of personal growth that stops people dead in their tracks. Surrendering how we view the world. Transforming how we think about who we are. Becoming open to seeing ourselves in a new and different way. Letting go of the ways we insulate ourselves from personal responsibility. That's a slippery slope for anyone to take on. It's a path that requires a lot of courage, a lot of patience, and a lot of hope that the future is better served in being on such a path.

What I ask people to do is challenge themselves to give up the ways they have insulated themselves from one essential truism of life. That truism has been the death knell of many persons' attempts at stepping out of the shadows. The truism: we are ultimately responsible for our emotional and spiritual well-being, a responsibility that can only be fulfilled by being grounded in the here-and-now.

To let that truism into our mind, body, and soul requires an important transformation to take place. We need to let go of the number one defense we all rely on, the number one way we stay frozen in the past, enslaved to the emotional storm that leaks into the here-and-now. The defense is, quite simply, blame.

We all recognize what blame is. It is displaced responsibility for our well-being. Blame is an accusation that communicates we feel hurt, betrayed, abandoned, abused, and humiliated by how we have been treated by others. But it leaves us stuck in the position of feeling perpetually wounded.

Paradoxically, blame is an anchor that keeps us stuck in our perception of previous acts of betrayal. It keeps us stuck for one very important reason. Blame is the conduit by which we give away our personal power. Blame is the means by which we surrender our ability to make the here-

and-now different. Blame is the source of toxic emotions that corrodes our spirit rather than empowers our journey.

The way we liberate ourselves from the perceptions clouded by the past is to take ownership of our thoughts, our feelings, and our actions. Another one of those simple things to say but hard things to do.

But that's the door we all have to walk through. We all have to develop a better understanding of who we are, what stirs us up, what our reactions mean rather than what we want them to mean.

We all need to cultivate a clearer understanding of what battles we are waging with the world as well as what their significance is. Do you understand what long-held wrongs you are trying to right with everyone who populates your here-and-now world? Can you see how you hold people in your life hostage to past events?

Getting clean in the present. Taking ownership. Letting go of the past. Does that give you a direction? Does that give you a sense of how to empower yourself by transforming your mindset? The transformation sounds something like this:

I will surrender the *mindset* of a victim for the mindset of a person who takes ownership of their actions.

I will surrender the *blissfulness* of ignorance for the emotional pain of self-awareness.

I will surrender the *ease of blame* for the sweat and toil of taking responsibility for my emotional and spiritual well-being.

I will surrender the *certitude* of living in the past for the uncertainty of living in the here-and-now.

I will surrender the *emotional safety* that comes from holding others responsible for my well-being for the discomfort provoked by living a life of integrity and accountability.

That's the roadmap I use when I feel like my past has overtaken my present. That's the compass I use when I feel I have become disoriented because I have handed responsibility to others for my well-being. That's the yardstick I use when I feel I have to measure whether I have strayed from where I want to be.

How about giving it a try. Why not write down some criteria for yourself? What are ways that you can measure whether your old mindset of blame, shifting responsibility, and not taking ownership of the here-and-now appear in your life? What are the transformations that need to take place within your mindset to insure that you are taking responsibility for the here-and-now?

This is big. It should not just roll off the tip of your pen. Give yourself plenty of time. If it feels like it is too overwhelming to do, do a little at a time. But whatever you do, don't walk away from it. The rewards will be worth the blood, sweat, and tears.

_____

_____

_____

_____

_____

_____

_____

_____

_____

_____

_____

_____
_____
_____
_____
_____
_____
_____
_____
_____
_____
_____
_____
_____
_____

If none of the above has been helpful to you, then just remember this one last thought. If someone comes up to you at a party and tells you you can't dance, it's time to stop blaming the band. How about looking into some dance lessons?

Opportunities Truly Are a Dime a Dozen

*The basic difference between an ordinary man
and a warrior is that a warrior takes everything
as a challenge, while an ordinary man takes
everything as a blessing or a curse.*

-Don Juan

Pathfinder's Tip

*Viewing our difficulties as opportunities will enable us to
transform our judgments into acceptance.*

"Damn! Damn! Damn! Damn!" I was muttering to
myself as I walked away from the ticket window.

I had just gotten the news that my train was going to
be late.

Even after taking a seat, I was still talking to myself,
"Late! Late! Late! Late! A thousand times it comes on
time. Today of all days it's late."

As I sat in my seat smoldering over the realization that
I had few choices and even fewer alternatives, a woman
sat down next to me.

"So do you know what time the train's coming?" she
asked.

"Train's late," I grunted back at her.

She smiled and said, "Yes I know, but do you know
when it's going to be here?"

"Ah, who cares?" I grumbled. Isn't it enough to
know it's late. Just see how they treat us. Other times,
nope, other times, it's never late. But today, of all days
it's late."

"You sound like it's personal," she said.

"It is personal. I have tomorrow off and now I can't
enjoy it."

"Now why would that be so?"

"Because now I'm in a bad mood and my bad moods last for days," I said in the most whining tone I could mustard up.

"Do you really think a train delay is personal, something done against you?" she inquired.

"Shouldn't I?" I responded.

"Why are you taking this so personally?" she asked still not understanding what was perfectly obvious to me.

"Because I am personally angry. And it's my personal life. And besides I'm just angry."

The weird thing was the angrier I got, the more she smiled at me. Finally I said to her, "Well, I'm glad this makes you laugh. I bet if my discomfort makes you happy then you would be rolling on the floor in hysterics if I fell and sprained my ankle."

"No," she explained, "I'm not laughing at you. It's just that I see so much of how I used to be in how you're acting right now. But I'm happy to say, I've changed my attitude about a lot of things."

"Oh, so what's your big secret?" I asked resenting her more and more.

"I don't know if it was any one thing or just a lot of little things. I guess I finally decided to accept that stuff just happens sometimes. Sometimes banks make mistakes. Sometimes my friends do me wrong. Sometimes things that I count on don't come out the way I want them to. And sometimes, sometimes trains are late."

She was finally getting my attention, so I started to soften my attitude towards her. "Well, what's your point?"

"My point is that you mustn't think you are the target or the victim of chance happenings. Even though you hurt, that doesn't mean someone is trying to hurt you."

"Do you really expect me to believe that this train that is about to delay my weekend and cause me untold amounts of misery and grief from the residual anger I will carry around all weekend is JUST A CHANCE THING THAT HAPPENED?" I asked starting to become exasperated all over again.

She didn't flinch as she said, "At least admit that it could be."

"But something caused this anger inside of me."

"Yes, I think something did," she said seriously, "I just don't think that it was as personal of an attack as you may feel it was."

"It's just late?" I asked somewhat in resignation.

"Yes, it's just late. If you are willing to listen, I have an idea about how to look at this whole late-train crisis thing," she shook back her hair as she spoke.

"Are you making fun of my crisis?"

"No, I'll save that for when I know you better. Anyway, do you want to hear my theory?"

"Okay, shoot."

"I think this train being late presented you with an opportunity that you might not have had otherwise."

"Oh really," I replied somewhat skeptically.

"Yes, really."

"Well then Ms. Know-It-All, what kind of opportunity might that be?"

"A brunette opportunity who usually doesn't talk to strangers."

"What, you? I bet you talk to everyone," I said.

"No, believe me I don't," she said while shaking her head. "It's just that you looked so upset and you were sitting there muttering to yourself."

"I was in a stupor or some kind of fit."

"I saw what you were doing, my point is that you mustn't see everything as a personal affront. Sometimes things aren't what they appear, sometimes they are tremendous opportunities disguised as disappointments."

"Should I think of you as a tremendous opportunity?" I asked somewhat hopefully.

"Let's just say that I am a jewel that you might never have seen if the train had been on time."

"So does that make me a tremendous opportunity for you?" I asked somewhat persistently.

"I don't know yet."

"When will you know?"

"When I give it some more thought."

"Can we sit together on the train?" I asked.

"Sure we can, but the train isn't going to be here for awhile."

"Well, when is the train going to be here?" I asked.

"Let's just say that meeting me is a bigger opportunity than you could have imagined."

Sometimes things aren't as they appear, they are an opportunity? Oh, come on now. We know exactly how to think about whatever happens to us. We are much practiced at interpreting the events of our life. We are well rehearsed at holding onto our point of view. We are battle tested at not letting go of our narrow mindedness. Clinging to our view of life, knowing what to make out of the events in our life is like an Olympic sport for most of us.

But to tell you the truth, the circumstances in our life are really opportunities dropped in our lap. Opportunities to transform our judgmental, self-critical ways of viewing life into one of compassion and understanding.

How so, you may be wondering. Simple.

We can accomplish so much by this singular act: transforming the way we think about the circumstances of our lives. The transformation? No longer thinking in terms of good or bad, right or wrong, perfect or worthless. No longer holding as our highest value winning or losing, being number one or being nothing at all.

No, the point of our journey is very different indeed. It's not the point to avoid mistakes and misdeeds. It's not the point of our journey to avoid hurt and disappointment.

We all need to embrace something different, a rule of thumb if you will. As we step out of the shadows, we will inevitably bump up against our limitations. Our journey is not about achieving spiritual perfection. We are here to learn about ourselves, who we are, how we react to life, where we fall short, how we can use who we are to expand ourselves.

Stepping out of the shadows is a process of adventure and experimentation. Seeing the circumstances in our life as opportunities provides the impetus we need to continue moving forward, not straying from our path of experimentation and adventure. Developing a mindset that interprets our life challenges as opportunities is the key to our cultivating personal growth.

How do we make such a transformation? Stop the judgments. Stop the personalizing. Stop the self-victimizing. Stop the demands for perfection. Release yourself from a quest that *judges* your humanness rather than *celebrates* it. Turn all of that in for one basic fundamental tenet: *all that the universe places in our path is an opportunity.* An opportunity to grow. An opportunity to learn. It's an opportunity to end the war that is waged within ourselves. End the war that is waged between life and ourselves. An opportunity to get our life back in harmony. Back in harmony with the true purpose for which we are here.

Simply by undergoing this transformation in how we view the world, we will discover that what the universe places in our path is an opportunity to look inward. To awaken our soul. To strengthen our spirit. To provide us with the necessary tests to sustain our faith.

This is how the universe illuminates our path. It tests us. The universe provides us with all we need to learn about ourselves, all we need do in order to expand our lives, as well as the consciousness with which we expand our lives. It's up to us to view those circumstances that the universe offers us as the means by which we grow or the means by which we are oppressed.

But the benefits go beyond what I have just mentioned. Imagine how the relationship you have with yourself will change by letting go of the criticalness that haunts our lives. The voice that never lets up on us, questioning what we do, how we do it. The voice that pushes us, beats us down, never lets us have a moment's peace.

No, the path to stepping out of the shadows is not a path of competition, competing with yourself or others. The relationship you have with yourself cannot be healed by living life by judgments. A path of genuineness can best be served when we view the people and the circumstances of our lives as opportunities, not as threats, not as proof of our worth, not as judgments of our value to the world.

Let's see if you, yourself, can discover the truth of what I am saying. Why not make a list of those circumstances that continue to appear in your life, circumstances that you experience as limiting or oppressive.

_____

_____

_____

_____

_____

_____

_____

_____

_____

_____

Now, let's see if there is some way to start thinking about these circumstances as an opportunity. How might it be that these obstacles may be the universe opening itself up to you and saying, "Here is something to help you learn about yourself and your journey?"

_____

_____

_____

_____

_____

_____

_____

_____

_____

_____

_____

_____

_____

_____

_____

_____

_____

_____

_____

_____

_____

_____

_____

_____

_____

_____

_____

_____

_____

_____

_____

This exercise can be an incredibly liberating exercise. Please give yourself the time to do it! Try and get to the point where it becomes automatic to think about the experiences in your life as opportunities. You will not always be able to see the opportunity in every happenstance of your life, but that doesn't mean there isn't one there for you. However, wouldn't you agree that even asking the question gives you a new choice? Afterall, that is the first step to personal freedom!

PART 6

Healing Your Wounds

I have only three enemies. My favorite enemy, the one most easily influenced for the better, is the British Empire. My second enemy, the Indian people, is far more difficult. But my most formidable opponent is a man named Mohandas K. Gandhi. With him I seem to have very little influence.

-Mohandas K. Gandhi

Healing on the Inside

You have no idea what a poor opinion
I have of myself—and how little I deserve it.

-W.S. Gilbert

He would lie awake at night thinking about what it would be like. Thinking about life without the nagging pain. The pain that permeated every cell of his body.

Laying alone there in the dark. Smoking cigarette after cigarette. Dwelling on how everyone else had wronged him. Holding onto every slight, real and imagined. Weaving a web of explanations and excuses.

"If only this, if only that," played in his head all night long. It didn't make the pain go away, but he couldn't imagine how much it would hurt without that familiar chorus playing in his head, numbing himself to what deep down inside he knew to be the truth, always finding some way to push it out of his mind.

As he drained another beer or downed another shot, he would make plans. Plans for a better tomorrow. Plans for a way to undo all the yesterdays of his life. Fantasy. Now that was a game he could play.

The nights that he hadn't drowned himself in cheap booze, self-pity was his drug of choice. He would shout at the top of his lungs, cursing the fates. Cursing them for not making him better than he was. For he never could shake the feeling of being damaged goods. No, that feeling had haunted him his whole life.

Defective didn't even begin to describe the feeling. Inadequate was just a quaint word to him. Worthless, well compared to the way he felt about himself, that didn't even make a dent in describing the relationship that he had with himself. No, you had to weave those three words together, almost invent a new word from the three to even begin to adequately describe the feelings he had about himself.

And this was the foundation of the relationship he had with himself. Not what the world could see. No a couple hours of sleep, a cold shower, and a little attitude, that was all he needed to shield the depth of his true feelings from you and me.

He had once read a book in which the author had used the word *toxic*. That would be a good beginning at trying to describe it. That seemed most accurate when he thought about the relationship that he had with himself. He laughed at all the cute phrases that were floating around in his culture. *Heal your inner child, learn to parent yourself, start to nurture yourself.* "Oh please, give me a break," he would think to himself.

Things seemed to be getting worse. He wasn't able to contain it the way he used to. He couldn't fake it anymore. As a kid, he would hide behind all the wildness, all of the false bravado. The only thing the bravado got him was more trouble than he could handle. It also left him believing more than ever that he was truly damaged goods.

If you asked him, I don't think he would be able to tell you that he was just plain scared, yet if you were at all conscious you couldn't miss it.

Some things settled down as he got older, but he never could shake the feeling that he didn't quite fit in. He bounced from job to job. Always feeling like an outsider, never quite trusting that anyone would want anything to do with him.

He masked that too. You see, he had become funny in a cute kind of way. So nobody thought to look beyond the jokes, always the soft ways he would put himself down.

The more the jobs didn't work out, the more convinced he was that there was something about him that just wasn't right. What were the words the books threw around? *Unhealthy. Dysfunctional.* "Yea, that's me," he figured.

"Oh, but when I become healthy, then I'll show 'em what I can be." That was the fantasy he retreated to more than anything else.

"I just have to fix me. I just have to figure out how to lose all of this."

Just what was *all of this*? Well, he never saw it as hurt. It never occurred to him that it was the pain of wanting so badly, needing so mightily, someone to be there for him. Pain and fear, what a combination that made; but no, it never entered his mind that that's what this was all about.

Could it have been the desperation of wanting to be loved but never letting anyone in? Maybe, but he couldn't tell you that. Don't leave out despair—the inevitable despair of not feeling accepted, or even acceptable for that matter. It just never occurred to him that this was all about being human.

He saw it as ugly, even petty. To him it was grotesque, something that was undesirable. The only truth it held for him was how ashamed he was of it, how he hid from it. The lump in his throat from all of the anger, bitterness, and resentments rolled up into one ball. All the humiliation he inflicted upon himself, all the fear he had of somebody else humiliating him, as well. Feeling like he never quite fit the bill. A feeling of emptiness that nothing he tried could fill.

This thing. It consumed him. It overtook his life. But not in any way that was obvious to you or me. What overtook his life was the way he tried denying that it was there. Bending it, twisting it, presenting it to the world in a way that might look acceptable. You would have never guessed the depth of what he was feeling, what he was hiding.

"Maybe, just maybe," you would have thought to yourself, "he just has to find himself."

But all along he thought something very different. "No way. There's no way they're going to pin anything on me. No one's going to discover what's buried in the depth of my soul. This *just feel your feelings crap.*" No it was much, much more important for him to push it all away.

He would have laughed at the idea that this was simply about being human. For being human couldn't hurt this much. He would have shrugged his shoulders if you would have tried to explain that his pain was really caused by his humanness being bent and distorted by his own fears, his own discomfort with his vulnerabilities.

He tried to make it go away. All those years he tried to pretend that it was never there. All those years he tried to numb himself to the experience of being human. Jumping in and out of relationships. Bouncing from job to job. Friends seemed to come and go, but mostly go.

The way he would explain it all? He would say that he was damaged. He would never have seen that it was him doing this to him. He would never have seen that he wasn't broken. Nothing about him was defective. Sure he was hurting, had hurt his whole life.

But most of that pain was of his own making. Most of the pain was self-inflicted. Most of the pain was born out of the relationship that he had with himself.

So, he never thought about his life as the experience of being human. Sadly, he could never see that what he believed to be the truth about himself—that he was broken and unhealthy—was merely the means by which he expressed his discomfort with being present in his life, experiencing all the terror that's part of being human. Sadly, he put most of his energies into attempting to fix the *problems* rather than accepting the experience of just being human.

There's nothing more toxic or more enriching to our emotional and spiritual well-being than the relationship we have with ourselves. Can you can see how the regard that we have for ourselves influences every aspect of our life?

Very simply, depending on the nature of the relationship we have with ourselves, we will:

- attract people who will either honor us or tear us down.
- create strong connections with the people in our life or alienate ourselves from those very people.
- actively create a life of fullness and meaning, or passively maintain a life of emptiness and despair.
- consistently shape our life to align with who we are, or live our lives following someone else's plan.

It's easy to see how our self-inflicted wounds poison us. We drift further and further away from our genuine self by investing more and more of our energy into keeping out of our conscious awareness who we genuinely are.

Our life becomes dedicated to masking the presence of those parts of ourselves that we hold judgments about. Much of our energy becomes focused on hiding from our awareness those things we judge to be unacceptable about who we are.

Along with a life created by our own self-condemnation, we oftentimes add to our feelings of self-alienation because of the powerlessness we feel about our inability to create our own life, to follow our own choices. We so burden ourselves with the prejudices we hold against ourselves that we lose our ability to distinguish between what is truth and what is our own self-critical judgments.

Do you recognize any of the following judgments?

❀We judge ourselves to be worthless and incapable.
❀We judge ourselves to be powerless and ineffective.
❀We judge ourselves to be small, frightened creatures who're incapable of exerting any influence to change from within.

From these judgments, it's only one small leap to making fact out of these fictions. Fictions that are merely a reflection of our own prejudices rather than an accurate assessment of what we're capable of. It's a tricky dance because we feel so strongly all of those things we believe to be true about ourselves. And when we feel it, we carry those feelings to their seemingly natural conclusion, we make *facts out of those feelings*.

As a result, we lose sight of our personal capabilities. We lose sight of our power. And ultimately, we lose sight of our path. We make our prejudices about ourselves law, and follow those laws accordingly. We become blinded by the fear our judgments create, we abdicate our ability to actively pursue our own journey. We become paralyzed with our own self-doubt and needlessly walk away from our path.

Can you see how this flows from the damage we inflict upon ourselves? Can you see how this flows from the relationship we've created with ourselves, based upon the judgments and the distortions we hold about ourselves?

You see, when we accept the fact that deep within we're whole and complete rather than broken and fragmented, then we're much better able to sustain the effort necessary to stay true to our path.

But the bottom line is that feelings aren't facts. We don't have to buy into the lies and distortions we can be subject to when we give more power to our emotions than we need give.

As we move on, it would be worth our while to pause for a moment to think about what we are discussing. Have you ever even considered that you have a relationship with yourself? What's the basis of that relationship? Is it a kind, affirming relationship? Is it a harsh, critical relationship? Is it the kind of relationship that's clouded with denial and rationalizations? What are the inner wounds that you need to heal?

_____

_____

_____

_____

_____

_____

_____

_____

_____

_____

_____

_____

_____

_____

_____

_____

_____

_____

_____

_____

_____

_____

The passageway to kindness and acceptance is healing your wounds. Kindness for yourself, acceptance for all the different pieces of the puzzle. This is where a shift needs to take place from within you about what's within you. No one can do this for you. Only you can provide the amount of love and understanding necessary to allow all of the different parts of who you are come together.

Just remember, out of this stage of the journey the promise for a new tomorrow will arise. A new tomorrow that's less harsh and chaotic. A new tomorrow that's more carefree and spontaneous. For as you heal the wounds that live within you, you will have also begun a life that's predicated upon openness and inclusion rather than secrecy and exclusion.

Judge Not and Ye Shall Not Be Judged

There are many who are living far below their possibilities because they are continually handing over their individualities to others. Do you want to be a power in the world? Then be yourself. Be true to the highest within your soul and then allow yourself to be governed by no customs or conventionalities or arbitrary man-made rules that are founded on principle.

-Ralph Waldo Emerson

Pathfinder's Tip

Accepting that we're imperfect beings rather than judging ourselves to be damaged goods is a necessary balm for creating a shift in the relationship we have with ourselves.

The night had been full of awe and wonder. I finally had visited Jodi's new home. I swear she had performed an absolute miracle. Forget that she had done most of the work herself. Forget that she had turned a shambles of a house into a majestic home.

No, the miracle was not that Jodi had pulled it off, because Jodi can do anything. The miracle in my mind was that she did it because of her unshakable belief in her vision, her unwillingness to forsake what was possible. She simply refused to be blinded by discouragement and hard times. She had pulled it off without the support of her family and friends. Indeed, they were some of the greatest obstacles she had to overcome.

You see, Jodi had found a house that was a handyman's dream. It wasn't in the greatest of neighborhoods, so anyone who cared about Jodi was dead set against her buying and rehabbing the house.

When she saw the house, all she could see was the potential it possessed. When her friends saw it, all they could see was how rundown it was. Friends would stare in horror at the condition of the house. Floors rotting away. Ceilings with holes in them the size of basketballs. Walls barely standing.

But all Jodi saw was what the house could become. The potential that existed in every nook and cranny. Jodi, ever the cock-eyed optimist, didn't see anything as being damaged; nope, everything in her mind, everything about the house was charm and character. Never mind the warped floor boards. Jodi never saw the destruction and decay, to her it was only the inevitable cycle of life evidenced throughout the entire 3000 square feet. Ruined. Hopeless. Daunting. Damaged. Irreparable. All ways her friends depicted the house.

But Jodi—Jodi never thought of the house in those terms. Never for a moment would she allow her spirit to be paralyzed, even infected by her friends' judgments. Potential. Possibilities. Style. Elegance. Warmth. Integrity. Those were her words. That was her vision.

Hard work. Don't talk to Jodi about hard work. With Jodi, hard work is always a given. Not because she has some twisted work ethic. She just understands that she always has to work to get to where she wants to be.

Well, the tour of the house was breathtaking. Although looking at the album of before and after pictures was boggling, nothing could recapture the smell of ruin that permeated that house only a short eight months ago. As we sat and talked, reliving the horror stories of the project, sharing the joy of Jody's vision coming to life, I was stumped. How could we have all been so wrong? All we could see was the destruction, yet she was able to see beyond what the house was in order to believe what the house could be.

So I asked Jodi. I asked her what her secret was. How could she have known that what she started with eight months ago would have turned into such a palace?

She pondered the question for a moment, cocked her head to one side and said, "I don't know. I guess I accepted the house for what it was. Never, ever did I dwell on what the house was not. Most importantly, I chose to see only the house for what it could become."

You know, that's not such a bad formula for how we might live our lives, for how we might relate to ourselves and the rest of the world.

How best to apply Jodi's principles for rehabbing a house to healing the relationship we have with ourselves? We need to accept that we're not broken; rather, we're imperfect beings who are growing and evolving.

To view ourselves as broken and in need of repair is the deepest, harshest wound we can inflict upon ourselves. Such a belief fuels and maintains our isolation from ourselves and the people in our lives. This wound keeps us hidden in the shadows because we limit the ways we feel safe in expressing who we are.

It's easy to see how this wound sends us into hiding, keeping us in the shadows. We hide from ourselves. We hide from the people in our life. We hide from our spiritual power.

Do you recognize what we are hiding from? Hiding from being found out. Hiding from being judged by others in the way we judge ourselves. Hiding from our fear. Our fear of not being liked and accepted, being rejected for all of the things we've already rejected about ourselves. So we tuck away those pieces of ourselves: you know the old adage, *out of sight out of mind*. Those pieces never to be claimed by ourselves, only to be disowned and unacknowledged.

And so the trauma perpetuates itself as we attempt to

dress our wounds. Do you recognize the ways we dress our wounds?

- We follow a path of self-condemnation rather than a path of celebration.
- We follow a path of judgment rather than a path of acceptance.
- We follow a path of repair rather than a path of discovery.
- We follow a path of achievement rather than a path of enlightenment.
- We follow a path of filling the emptiness created by our wounds rather than a path of filling our soul with love and forgiveness.

No, it must be plain to us all by now, that we must forsake many of the ways we've gone about the business of healing.

- Healing does not come from filling the void with the trappings of our culture.
- Healing does not come from the temporary means we have to soothe ourselves.
- Healing does not come from smothering our pain in our compulsions.
- Healing does not come from the emotion-numbing experiences of drugs and alcohol.
- Healing does not come from the ways we lose ourselves in work, achievement, and self-destructive relationships.

How does healing take place? Hopefully there's a glimmer stirring here, an understanding of how to go about creating healing within ourselves.

❀ Healing arises out of the shift we experience in the relationship we have with ourselves.

❀ Healing arises out of our willingness to absolve ourselves from the judgments we hold against ourselves.

❀ Healing arises out of our willingness to let go of the impossible standards we hold ourselves to.

❀ Healing arises out of our willingness to let ourselves become what we were meant to be.

❀ Healing arises out of creating a wholeness within.

Does any of this have a ring of truth for you? Have you taken pause to think about whether you think of yourself as damaged goods? Are you able to see that we all are evolving creatures that are growing towards our highest possibilities?

I have a simple exercise that I suggest people do. Its aim is also simple: forgiveness. More specifically, forgiving ourselves.

The mechanism for forgiveness? Release ourselves from the harshness that lives in the relationship we have with ourselves. Release ourselves from the contempt we feel towards ourselves for what we're not. Release ourselves from the voices within that ridicule us, demean us, that ride us unmercifully.

The following exercise may feel awkward at first, but don't give up on it. For this exercise can be the starting point for something very important. We need to learn how to talk to ourselves in a kind, soothing, healing way. To heal our relationship with ourselves, we need to develop a different way of treating ourselves. That's the practical side of this exercise.

But the healing aspect of this exercise is what I want each and every one of you to experience. Take your time with this one. If you skip over it now, promise yourself that you'll come back later.

What I want each and every one of you to do is to write a letter of forgiveness to yourself. Let me break this down for you.

Start off by making a list of what you feel you need to forgive yourself for. Not being smart enough? Not being attractive enough? Not being kind enough? Whatever the judgments you hold against yourself, whatever you beat yourself up for, these are the things that you need to release yourself from.

_____

_____

_____

_____

_____

_____

_____

_____

_____

_____

_____

_____

_____

_____

_____

_____

_____

_____

_____

Now look at the list. Remember Jodi's formula? *I guess I accepted the house for what it was. Never, ever dwelled on what the house was not. More importantly, I chose to see only the house for what it could become.*

Take your list and apply Jodi's formula. Write yourself a letter of forgiveness wherein you change your judgments into a vision of what's possible for you to become.

_____

_____

_____

_____

_____

_____

_____

_____

_____

_____

_____

_____

_____

_____

Let me emphasize the following one last time. Hopefully, you're beginning to discover the empowerment of transforming how you think about things. Healing your own self-inflicted wounds is another step towards empowering your life. We no longer need to injure ourselves by the way we hold our imperfections in our head. Just remember the next time you begin to go off on yourself, exercise a little kindness as well. It's just as easy to forgive as it is to belittle yourself.

Give to Ourselves What We Gladly Give to Others

*Compassion for myself is the most powerful
healer of them all.*

-Theodore Isaac Rubin

Pathfinder's Tip

*Healing will envelop our soul as we embrace
the belief "I deserve."*

"Why do I keep putting myself in these situations? It seems like I'm always setting myself up for a big fall! Every time I think that there's the slightest glimmer of hope, the slightest reason to believe that I'm changing things around for myself, boom, I fall right back into the same old destructive setup."

Mikey and I were taking our Sunday walk along the lakefront, talking about the ways we manage to trip over ourselves.

"Mikey, what happened?" I asked.

"I really thought I was better able to see it coming this time. I thought I understood all I needed to understand so that it wouldn't happen again."

"Understand what, Mikey?" I asked, still not understanding anything.

"I thought by figuring it out, I wouldn't step back into it, you know what I mean?"

"No, I don't know what you mean," I told Mikey.

"I thought I had fixed me, but I still keep falling back. Wouldn't you think that just once, I would be with someone who cared about me for me. But noooo, I always set things up so that I find someone who needs me, but doesn't have a clue about how to care about me.

"Sure, I know all the signs, but time after time, I find myself right back in the circle. I know I feel safest when I'm needed. I know I believe the only reason anyone would want anything to do with me is because I'm like a loyal St. Bernard, always coming to the rescue. I know I should believe that someone could actually value me for me but noooo, have you ever seen me try that tact before?"

I was running out of ways to get Mikey to explain to me what happened, so I just went along with his soliloquy.

"No, Mikey, I've never seen you try that tact before."

"And do you know why that is?"

"No, Mikey, why?"

"Because, I can't picture myself being with someone without all the chaos, without all the noise that goes with being needed. I know my part in that drama real well.

"But I would be lost in any other play. I think I would be second-guessing myself a lot, you know questioning myself. You know why that is, don't you?"

"No, Mikey, why?

"'Cause I just can't get past these feelings that I don't deserve it any other way. These feelings that it can't possibly be any other way, that I can't be any other way."

"Mikey, come on man, what the hell's this all about?"

"As long as I'm pouring all of my attention and energy into my partner, it's draining and it's lonely. But you know what, the truth of the matter is, it's safe as hell. I don't have to risk very much. Well, at least, risk having to show myself to anyone else.

"You know what the real truth is, Steve?"

"Mikey, I lost sight of that ten minutes ago."

"The truth is I don't know how to let someone care about me. I think I would crawl right out of my skin.

Answer me this—just how do you let someone care about you when you don't believe you deserve it, when you feel like everything in this world carries a price tag, that things are bought and paid for but never simply offered and received?"

"Mikey, I don't know how to answer that, but you know man, I care about you."

"Yea, yea. I know and I appreciate that, I really do. But you know what, I don't always feel right about that either. There were times that I just didn't feel like I deserved it. Man, it's hard to explain. But to be honest with you, that's why I used to disappear so much. I just couldn't let it in for too long, still can't really."

"I always knew how hard it was for you, that's why I would back off, as well. But, we got past that."

"Yea, but I can't get past that with the women in my life.I feel so trapped. On one hand, I keep setting myself up to take care of the world and then when the world doesn't give me anything back, I become angry and resentful. On the other hand, I don't dare try to do it any differently because I'm afraid of letting anyone be there for me.

"I'm afraid that I'll be a disappointment to them, that they'll be put off by who I am. Even if they get through that maze, I just don't feel like I deserve to be cared about."

Mikey is a prisoner of his emotional needs and how he chooses to get them met. The thing that Mikey is unable to tap into is a sense of entitlement. But you know one of the most profound shifts that I witness most people go through is precipitated by letting into their lives two little words, *I deserve*. When those two words become a part of our heart and soul, we can move mountains.

These two simple words can set us free from the messages we feed ourselves. The messages that ooze from the toxins that infect the wounds we have inflicted upon ourselves. The messages that limit our opportunities to grow and become who we're most capable of being.

I never cease to be amazed at the power that these two words hold for us once we embrace them with all of our being. Think about it for a moment.

Do you embrace with all of your being the fact that you're deserving of a life that's an expression of who you are?

Do you embrace with all of your being that you're deserving of a life that fills you with an abundance of love and support?

Do you embrace with all of your being that you're deserving of a life that reflects who you are rather than what you're afraid of being?

Do you embrace with all of your being that you're deserving of having people in your life who support rather than undermine your well-being?

Can you see how the process of healing is developing an unabiding belief—a belief that we're deserving of the things we dare to dream about? Can you see how believing *we're deserving* will bring an end to the tyranny of worthlessness that we've imposed upon ourselves?

Let's take this a step further.

Do you recognize what your own self-imposed limits are?

Do you recognize the areas of your life that cause you pain because you deny that you deserve it to be any different?

Do you recognize how your life's a perpetual conflict between what you want and what you allow yourself to have?

Do you recognize how not believing you deserve to become who you were meant to be keeps you hidden in the shadows?

Has any of this struck a chord with you? If so, it helps to do more than make a passing nod at the questions. Putting things down on paper makes things more concrete, more difficult to ignore. Do yourself the favor of learning something about how you deny yourself, how you deny your very destiny.

Write down how your life is affected by not maintaining the belief *I deserve.*

_____

_____

_____

_____

_____

_____

_____

_____

_____

_____

_____

_____

_____

_____

_____

_____

_____

_____

_____

_____

_____

_____

_____

_____

_____

_____

_____

_____

_____

_____

_____

_____

_____

_____

Now it's time to create a vision. A very special vision. A vision that deserves your special consideration. A vision of what your life would be like if you sprinkled your life with those two simple yet powerful words, *I deserve.*

_____

_____

_____

_____

_____

_____

_____

_____

_____

_____

_____

_____

_____

_____

_____

_____

_____

_____

_____

_____

_____

_____

_____

Is there a solution to all that we have denied ourselves? The same simple act I mentioned in the last chapter. The act? It's so fundamental to our growth, it bears being mentioned again and again and again. Forgiveness! Forgiveness! Forgiveness! There's no getting away from it.

Are you starting to see the link between forgiving ourselves and believing we deserve all those things our journey offers us? Don't be fooled by this simple step. Many of us will push it away. Many of us will fight its impact upon our lives. Many of us will even question the necessity of taking this step.

I watch how people discard this simple step for something that is more palatable or more profound in its complexity. But rarely have I seen a person who fought the idea of forgiving themselves, not eventually come around to seeing the wisdom of forgiving themselves.

And the truth of the matter is, it will likely happen exactly that way for you as well.

Rearranging Our Priorities

In the midst of winter, I discovered an invincible summer.

-Albert Camus

Pathfinder's Tip

We will experience a shift in the relationship we have with ourselves when we start healing our insides rather than trying to change who we are on the outside.

My grandfather loved to tell us stories when we were growing up. He was one of those guys that thought that everything should have a lesson to it and he was the one who was going to teach us those lessons. Every story had a moral to it that he wanted us to learn, so he would lecture us for hours on end after telling us one of his stories.

This is a story he once told about a young girl who possessed great joy and beauty. She lived on a small farm in a simple house. Several times a week she would go to town to buy food for the family.

Every time she came to town people spoke to her. Her spirit had an unusual way of attracting people.

For example, the woman who worked at the market would often say to her, "My dear, your eyes are so pretty today, they glimmer with a natural beauty. I was saying to Mrs. Hobbs next-door just this morning, that you may soon catch a husband without ever enhancing your eyes with shadow at all. Of course, can you imagine how much more attractive you might appear to a man if you put on a beautiful shadow?"

The young girl would nod her appreciation and leave.

The next time the girl would come to the market, the woman might comment on her hair. For instance she would ask, "Is it difficult to braid your hair? Your hair seems so course and bleached by the rays of the sun. I have noticed that the times you tie your hair with a ribbon and bow, large curls form as it falls around your shoulders. I was thinking that such conditions might make your hair unmanageable and difficult to control. Is that true?"

"Not really. I just let it be what it will be," the girl replied.

"Of course you do, dear," said the woman. "I imagine that will change when you want to show the world who you really are. When you want more from life."

"Why would it change?" asked the girl.

"Because you will want to be really beautiful!" said the woman. "Everyone knows that beauty comes from appealing to what *others* want. When you are ready, come to my house, then I will make you beautiful."

The girl spent the evening thinking about what the woman from the market said to her. Never before had she looked outside herself to find beauty, but what if there was a special secret she didn't know. After all, she was still single and lived with her parents while most of the women of the town were married with homes of their own.

After thinking about the market woman's offer for several months, the girl finally relented and went to the woman to ask that she make her beautiful.

The woman gathered all her friends and together they set out to make the girl beautiful. She instructed her friends, "Her hair has to be parted and pulled back tight."

Then it was decided to lace the girl's hair with vines and dried flowers.

Feeling that the job was not just right, the woman added a small stuffed bird.

Next they went to work on her face. Now the instructions were, "Her face should be painted white with powder and then red on the cheeks to stimulate the golden rays of the sun. Finally, we must cover her in perfume that will attract men."

When the girl returned home later her mother had a fit. Her brother laughed. Her father was silent with shock.

Embarrassed by her family's reactions, the girl avoided going into town over the winter months. Finally, by spring most of the makeup had worn away.

On returning to town in the spring, the woman at the market greeted her with shock.

"My dear, what has happened to you? When I last saw you, you were beautiful, the way we had made you up. Now you are only a simple farm girl again."

The girl replied, "I can only be who I am. Everything I add to try and change myself, only takes something away. I appreciate your help. Your intentions were good, but I have learned that to change so much I have to forfeit who I am.

"As I lived through this winter season, I thought to myself how complex this change really was. The outside is where it began, but I felt like I would have to lose myself on the inside in order to be able to keep the masquerade going.

"I would need to change my attitudes and feelings until soon they were not mine at all, but rather attitudes and feelings of someone else. In the end, by changing myself on the outside I would not be me on the inside, I would simply be an imitation of someone else.

"This winter taught me to be happy with who I am on the inside and leave the outside alone."

With that the woman in the market never said another word to the girl. She merely sold her goods and watched as she came and went.

The girl did quite well on her own.

Now this is one of the oldest messages in the world. But, for how many of us is this one of the oldest traps in the world as well? We are inundated everyday with messages for products that profess to hold the magic to our physical and emotional well-being. And there's just no escaping these messages.

But the truth of the matter is, no matter how much we toy with the externals, it's our insides that we need to bring honor to. Without the proper appreciation for who we are and what we are becoming, there's nothing that can free us from the shadows.

Much of the work we've done to this point has really focused on that very point. Awakening. Liberating. Honoring. Reclaiming. Transforming. All means at our disposal for one thing and one thing only.

Celebrating who we are, rather than abandoning our very essence. Claiming the Truth about ourselves rather than turning to prescriptions to bury that Truth. Embracing a path of forgiveness and acceptance rather than clinging to our critical and judgmental ways.

There's an important point to all of these experiences. To experience the sense of wonder and joy that lives within. But more importantly, these experiences and consequent feelings of joy and wonder can only be created by ourselves.

When I talk about our need to experience a shift in the relationship we have with ourselves, that shift will occur only when we turn our gaze inward. To not only turn inward, but to celebrate what we discover about ourselves as well.

Let's end this section on a positive note of encouragement and hope. It's important to connect with those parts of yourself that need to be recognized and honored. Too often we spend our time focused on those parts of ourselves that we don't cherish, those parts we believe we have to fix or make disappear. The way I do this is regularly writing a *Letter of Thanks*.

That's right, I express my gratitude to those parts of myself that have shown themselves to me. I honor those parts for what they are, how they appear in my life, and how wonderfully they serve me. Perhaps my courage has gotten me through a difficult project. Or my anger has protected me from something that was frightening me. Or my playfulness has rescued me from too much work. Perhaps my sense of humor has brought sanity to an otherwise crazy situation. Perhaps my ability to love has brought care and comfort to somebody else.

My point is, how often do we take the time to express gratitude to ourselves for who we are? This exercise is a way of providing equal time for all the air play we give to our critical voice inside.

This is one of those exercises that picks up power and steam the more it's done. Give this one some thought, for many of us may not be used to exercising our thoughts about ourselves in such a way. However, the more time you give to this exercise, the more automatic it will become in your day-to-day life.

_____

_____

_____

_____

_____

_____

_____

_____

_____

_____

_____

_____

_____

_____

_____

_____

_____

_____

_____

_____

The secret to this tip is the notion of inward celebration. When I mention this in the Relationship Bridge-Building groups, people roll their eyes at me, but it works, and I know it works, most importantly they have discovered that it works. Quite simply, we all need to develop an *attitude of gratitude* with regard to ourselves.

How best to live the *attitude of gratitude*? Discover the majesty of who you are rather than search for temporary solutions for the things that you are not.

PART 7

Strengthening the Bonds
of Fellowship

*Now is the Law of the Jungle—
as old and as true as the sky;
And the Wolf that shall keep it may prosper
but the Wolf that shall break it must die.
As the creeper that girdles the tree trunk,
the Law runneth forward and back—
For the strength of the Pack is the Wolf,
and the strength of the Wolf is the Pack.*

-Rudyard Kipling

$\mathcal{A}$ Prescription for Emotional and Spiritual Well-Being

There comes that mysterious meeting in life when someone acknowledges who we are and what we can be, igniting the circuits of our highest potential.

- Rusty Berkus

"Thanks for seeing me after group tonight, I just need a couple of minutes of your time."

Laurie asked to see me for a few minutes after our group session in order to discuss a recommendation her doctor had made for her.

"I got a physical today and my doctor started asking me a bunch of questions. The next thing I knew, she was telling me she thought it would be a good idea for me to start taking antidepressant medication.

"I told her I thought that I should talk it over with you first."

I spent a few minutes talking with Laurie about the research on antidepressant medication, the pros and cons, what her choices were.

The one thing I emphasized with Laurie, as I do with all of my clients is, as a clinical psychologist I cannot pre-scribe medication. However I was more than happy to share with her a prescription that I can and do *write* for all of my clients.

She seemed to perk up a little when I told her that, so I continued.

"There are three things that I prescribe for anybody who is struggling, trying to enhance their emotional well-being. The first thing I prescribe is *people*. We have to step out of our isolation and find a way to get connected to the human race. There's nothing more healing to the soul than to experience the love and the support we can get only from being involved with other human beings.

"It's really very simple. We all need to feel like we have

a place in this world, that we matter to another living soul, that we hold some importance to somebody else. The relationship we have with ourselves is important for our emotional well-being, but that relationship has its own limits."

Laurie was listening intently to what I had to say. She was nodding her head as I was speaking, so I continued.

"The second thing I prescribe is *people*. We need to be able to step out of our own problems, out of our own pain, and contribute, contribute to somebody else's life. Involvement with other people, providing emotional nutrition for somebody else is a magical elixir for our own frozen souls.

"When we isolate and disconnect from our world, we feel empty as our lives are void of meaningful contact with others. Feeling alienated from the rest of the world drains our spirit of hope and purpose, the thought that our life matters. The act of giving to others, the act of transcending our own constricted world, plants the seeds of hope and purpose in our own lives."

Laurie was still with me, so I looked at her and asked, "Now those are the first two things that I prescribe, what do you imagine the third thing is?"

Laurie stuck her right index finger under her chin, tilted her head back a little, rolled her eyes toward the ceiling, smiled and asked, "Uh, it wouldn't be *people*, would it?"

"As a matter of fact, it would be. People is the third thing I prescribe. We need to be involved with *people* who are emotionally safe for us. People who can be supportive, who can be there for us. Emotionally safe relationships are an important catalyst for our own personal growth. They provide the necessary contact we need with others to get out of ourselves. People who are emotionally safe to be with provide an outlet for us to step out of our woundedness and experiment with how we live our lives.

"That's the essence of our emotional and spiritual well-being. Experimentation. Experimenting with our life choices. Expanding the world in which we live. Plugging into the love and support from others who are invested in our development, not threatened by it."

Strengthening the Bonds of Fellowship. That's what I call this stage of our journey. Building bridges to the human race. Getting involved with the people in our lives. Ending the wars we wage not only within ourselves, but with all the people we come into contact with.

Ending the isolation. Transforming the alienation. Creating harmony where there was once acrimony and pain. Does that sound like fertile ground to march upon?

Do you see the value of fellowship in the context of the big picture we're painting? Here's how I think about it. Relationships are like a mirror. A mirror that reflects back to us who we are, and who we can become. A mirror from which we can learn how the world experiences us, which invariably is different than what we believe to be true about ourselves.

Without a consistent source of contact with safe people that we can learn to be ourselves with, we lose an important balancing point to the many judgments we hold about who we are. Creating meaningful contact with safe people provides us with important feedback so that we may escape our self-imposed prisons of alienation and condemnation.

Let me more specifically list for you the value I find in all of us being willing and able to strengthen the bonds of fellowship. Don't just read the list, but think about how any one item may hold some truth for you.

- ❀Emotionally safe relationships enhance our self-esteem.
- ❀Emotionally safe relationships activate the seeds of our potential for our personal growth.
- ❀Emotionally safe relationships extract ourselves from the darkness of our isolation.
- ❀Emotionally safe relationships elevate our mood.
- ❀Emotionally safe relationships enable us to contribute to the well-being of other people.
- ❀Emotionally safe relationships enable us to see more clearly how the world experiences us.
- ❀Emotionally safe relationships create a purpose in our lives.
- ❀Emotionally safe relationships teach us about who we are.

Let's stop for a moment and explore in a more personal way what *Strengthening the Bonds of Fellowship* means to you. Try to focus on the value you can add to your life by building better bridges with the people who matter most to you.

_____

_____

_____

_____

_____

_____

_____

_____

_____

_____

_____

_____

_____

_____

_____

_____

_____

_____

_____

_____

_____

_____

_____

_____

As I share with you my prescription for emotional well-being, I am not naive enough to believe that it's not without its own set of side-effects. That's why we work so hard in our Relationship Bridge-Builders groups to develop the skills and the awarenesses necessary to insure that we create safe relationships. At the same time, on balance throughout the years, I have discovered that there's not a more powerful elixir than safe relationships that support our growth and accept who we are and where we are at in our journey.

'Tis Best to Receive As Well As to Give

We are each of angels with only one wing.
And we can only fly embracing each other.

-Luciano de Crescenzo

Pathfinder's Tip

Our fellowshipping is strengthened by transcending the obstacles we create for others in becoming our friend.

"Kojak, you stay away from me now, ya hear? I told you I don't want you coming around here, *shrinking my head.*"

Lanis was starting the dance that we went through everytime he'd see me drive up to the house. At the time, I was working at a halfway house for men who were homeless after being released from prison. Lanis was on my caseload. From the time we first met, he called me Kojak. When I asked him why, he would just nod his head, give me one of his conspiratorial smiles and say, "Ah come on now, Kojak, you know why I call you that."

Anyway, today was no different than any other day. He would be standing around the court yard. He would see me drive up, wait till I got within twenty-five feet of him, start shouting at me, then walk away. But he never walked away fast enough so that he would lose me. We always wound up in the same place where we would then sit and talk for at least an hour.

Today, I especially wanted to talk to him because I had a gift for him. I had noticed that Lanis had been limping the last few weeks. When I asked him about it, he would just shrug it off. After a while, I could tell that his left shoe had developed a huge hole in the sole, so I found him a new pair of shoes to get him through the impending Chicago winter.

When I gave Lanis the shoes, he spent ten minutes trying to convince me that he didn't need anything from me.

"Kojak, I keep telling you to stay away from me. Now you go and do this. What's the matter with you? Why do you keep bothering me like this?"

"You think I'm bothering you?"

"Well, yea man. Why do you keep trying to get in my face? I don't need you or anything you have to offer me!"

"Lanis, why do you keeping acting like you're so bad with me all the time? What are you so afraid of?"

"Hey man, I just don't want you getting too close to me, is that alright with you, Kojak, or do you have to make a big deal out of that too?"

"I'm not making a big deal out of anything, but I just don't get why it's so hard for you to accept someone's kindness."

"Listen Kojak, I can't figure you out, but I know you've got an angle here, I just can't figure out what angle you're shooting."

"Is it impossible to believe that the only angle I have is a concern for you or maybe even having a friendship with you. Have you ever considered that angle?"

"Kojak, don't even go there, don't you try that stuff with me. I know different. I know that everybody wants something from somebody. Nobody does something for nothing."

"What's the matter, Lanis? You think you'll be obligated to me if you accept my kindness? You think I'll hit up on you for something just because you accept my concern?"

241

"That's the way of the world, Kojak, don't pretend it's any different. I'll take these damn shoes from you, but don't you try and sell me on anything different, 'cause it just ain't so."

How many of us recognize the struggle that Lanis experienced with me?

Wanting to have people in our lives, but uncomfortable with letting anybody in.

Wanting to accept the kindness of somebody else, but not trusting enough to accept their kindness.

Wanting to feel connected to somebody else, but fearful of the price for allowing that to happen.

Think for a moment about the obstacles you construct to keep people from getting close. Do you recognize how people may come knocking on your door only to be pushed away by you? Take a moment and think about it. What are some of the scenarios that appear in your life in which people reach out to you, only to be sidestepped by you?

_____

_____

_____

_____

_____

_____

_____

_____

_____

_____

_____

_____

What experience has taught me is that we all have our reasons to keep people at arm's length. Invariably, there are some fears that we hold about letting people in, letting people see us up front and personal.

For some, it could be that in the past we've had bad experiences.

Perhaps we've let people get close to us and they've used what they've learned about us against us.

Perhaps we've experienced humiliation as a result of letting somebody get too close.

Perhaps we've been taken advantage of by others. People continually taking from us without us experiencing any kind of reciprocity in return.

It could be that we feel frail on the inside. And in feeling frail, we feel our only option is to keep people at a distance.

Self-worth has a lot to do with this. Do we feel like we deserve the kindness of others? Do we feel like friendships are something we are entitled to?

These are but a few of the reasons we keep people at a safe distance, pushing them away, rebuffing their advances.

But let's take a moment and see what the truth is for you. What makes it hard for you? What are the fears that you walk around with as they relate to the way you're in your relationships?

_____

_____

_____

_____

_____

_____

Don't lose sight of what we're trying to accomplish. Quite simply, we want to strengthen our connection to the human race. We want to open ourselves up to being present with people in all aspects of our life. The payoff is enormous, the price we pay when we're disconnected is proportionately high, as well.

The bottom line is that fellowship is a two-way street. If we don't feel comfortable being a friend to others, it's unlikely that we'll make it comfortable for others to be a friend to us.

The more discomfort we have with extending ourselves to others, it's likely that others will experience a similar discomfort when they extend themselves to us.

The key to allowing people into our world is to become more skilled in entering other people's world. I've seen it happen time and time again. That perhaps is the most important skill a person develops in my Relationship Bridge-Builders groups.

The more comfortable a person becomes with offering themselves to another person, the more comfortable they also become in allowing others to be a friend to them. It's just like I said earlier, if you want people to be in your life, first master the art of being a friend to them. That's one side of the coin of strengthening the bonds of fellowship. The other side is feeling comfortable enough to let somebody in when they come-a-knocking.

Just like me and Lanis: remember the choice Lanis created for himself? You can continue to limp through life by yourself wearing shoes with holes in them or you can extend your hand to someone when they extend their hand to you!

PART 8

The Rhythm of Life

In order to arrive at what you do not know
You must go by a way which is the way of ignorance
In order to possess what you do not possess
You must go by the way of dispossession
In order to arrive at what you are not
You must go through the way in which you are not.
And what you do not know is the only thing you know
And what you own is what you do not own
And where you are is where you are not.

-T.S. Elliot

Hi-ho, Hi-ho, It's Off to Work We Go

It is good to have an end to journey toward,
but it is the journey that matters in the end.

-Ursula LeGuin

We will need a way of maintaining our bearings as we undertake the transformation explored in this book. The means is simple. We only need to understand and come to trust *The Rhythm of Life.*

I hope by now you have a better appreciation for what goes into stepping out of the shadows, but do you understand that it's a process that unfolds over a lifetime? As you discover what each passageway in this book looks like for you, you'll next discover that life is nothing more than a process of experimentation. Simply put, there's an ebb and flow to whatever you do. You will not do even a majority of this work *right.*

But that's not the point. The only *right* thing to do is to keep on trying. Don't approach this work like it's one more thing you need to excel at, because I promise you, you won't. You'll struggle because it's part of the human condition to struggle.

But there are ways to be with your struggle that will inch you closer and closer to your destiny. A destiny in which you'll be free to be who you want to be. A destiny full of purpose and well-being. A destiny that leaves you healed from within, connected on the outside with the people who matter most, and aligned from above with a higher power.

The tools of such a destiny? Take these two with you. Choice and risk-taking. Throw perfectionism out the window. Open yourself up to what's possible. Transform your life with these two trustworthy means: your freedom to make choices and the courage to take risks. These are the pick and shovel for the work we must all do in order to step out of the shadows.

Pathfinder's Compass

*Stepping out of the shadows begins with our
willingness to "let go."*

The process of stepping out of the shadows needs to
be sprinkled with *a little bit of this* and *a little bit of that*.
The little bit of this is flexibility and joy. These are the two
ingredients that we'll use to replace rigidity and idealism.
Although I have presented you with my slant of how our
journey will unfold, please leave this experience knowing
that there's no *one* right way. I've only attempted to provide you with the chalklines that outline the playing field.
It'll be up to you to create the rules of the game and what
position you want to play.

I only hope that we can agree on the general outcome.
Joy. Wonder. Renewal. Exultation. Transformation.

Now the *little bit of that* is letting go. I have the following quote by Andre Gide taped on my desk as a
never-ending reminder of the importance of letting go.
"One doesn't discover new lands without consenting to
lose sight of the shore for a very long time."

We can't transcend where we are in our lives without
the willingness to live the spirit of this quote. Think about
it for a moment. What new lands do you wish to visit?

_____

_____

_____

_____
_____
_____
_____
_____
_____
_____
_____
_____
_____
_____
_____
_____
_____
_____
_____

At the same time, can you see how whatever it is you're clinging to prevents you from visiting those new lands? Again, give this some careful consideration. What *shores* do you need to let go of in order that you may visit *new lands?*

_____
_____
_____
_____
_____
_____
_____
_____
_____
_____

Letting go is unavoidable and oftentimes quite painful. But letting go is one of those things that, quite simply, is a note of the rhythm of life. As much pain as it brings, it opens our life up to new and wondrous things at the same time. Just like that old saying, *for every door that closes, a new one opens,* letting go is the mechanism by which we discover new pieces of the puzzle, new parts of ourselves, and, most importantly, new ways of being in the world.

Pathfinder's Compass

*[Re]connecting to our life's journey requires that we give
more to the journey than the journey gives back to us.*

"I've tried everything, believe me, none of this works.
I've been in and out of therapy for over ten years. I med-
itated for two years."

"Every day, twice a day?" I asked.

"Well no, not exactly. It didn't seem to be working the
way I thought it should, so I just did it here and there.

"I've tried three different twelve step programs. None,
I mean none of that stuff helped. All of those people
bitching and complaining. All that God stuff."

"Did you try to find a meeting with people who you
liked?" I asked.

"Not exactly. But..."

"Did you get anybody's phone number so you could
get some support from them?" I asked.

"Not exactly. But..."

"Did you go to any one meeting long enough so that
you could get a sponsor?"

"Not exactly. But..."

"Did you learn how to work the steps?"

"Not exactly. But, I did buy three books on how to do
the steps," he said somewhat defensively.

"Did you read the books?"

"Not exactly. I could see those programs weren't for

me. I tried group therapy, but that didn't work either."

"Did you try and connect with the people in the group?"

"Not exactly. But..."

"Did you go to the group every week?"

"Not exactly. But..."

"Did you ask the group leaders for help?"

"Not exactly."

"Well, just what exactly is it that you're waiting for, some sort of guarantee that all of this stuff works before you try to do what you're supposed to do?"

How many times have we built up a big head of steam about something, new yet never move beyond square one? A new exercise program, a new food plan, checking out a few classes at the local college. What about the musical instrument we promised ourselves we were going to learn how to play?

No matter what process of transformation we become involved with, bear in mind this very simple formula: what we receive from any person or thing will be in direct proportion to what we invest in that person or thing. Makes sense. Nothing terribly profound about it. But?

How many of us can honestly say that we give more to an experience than what we expect to receive from it? Yet, it's this very principle we need to embrace in order to gain the very benefits we hope to derive.

So often, I see people quit in discouragement. Their discouragement given birth by their belief that someone or something has failed them. They walk away in discouragement, ignoring the simple law that can assure them an abundance of whatever it is that they're seeking.

Fess up now, is any of this true for you? Looking for resources, wanting to know what those resources will do for you, but not willing to invest yourself in what the process requires of you. Does that ring true for you? Placing all of your hopes and dreams in the next book, the next workshop, the next quick-fix remedy, but never taking the time to understand what's required of you.

What does it mean to *invest yourself*? In its most simplistic terms, show up, be present, participate. Know that any means of transforming your life is not a passive process. It's a process that requires you to give of yourself in a consistent fashion. Don't just give when you're hurting and scared. Don't just give when you're feeling particularly inspired. Don't just give when you're feeling particularly rewarded for your efforts.

Every day, take the next small step. Do the next thing that you know you need to do. Don't wait for what you want to present itself to you. If you keep looking for the immediate reward, for some sense of why you should keep-on-keeping-on, even when there's no immediate justification for doing so, then you have only set yourself up to fail.

Be prepared to feel frustrated from time to time. Know that it'll be more tempting to hold others responsible for your well-being rather than take responsibility for your well-being. But that shall pass as you find new ways to get around old obstacles.

Remember, pain is what gets most of us involved in this kind of work, but it's not what will keep us involved.

Pathfinder's Compass

*[Re]connecting to our life's journey is built
upon the efforts of honestly exploring who we are in
the context of ourselves, our friends and family,
and our place in the universe.*

Our unfinished business lives within the above quote.
Until we honestly seek to bring understanding and acceptance where all is now denial and pain, we'll be doomed to
live a life stuck in a web of our yesterdays.

Does that make sense to you? We can't grow beyond
the experiences of our past until we put to bed the ghosts
of the past. It's a simple rule of thumb about the rhythm
of life. The work that lies before us is going nowhere until
we meet it head on and work *through* it, otherwise it will
reappear in our lives over and over again.

This is the most fundamental premise of my
Relationship Bridge-Builders groups. It's a safe environ-
ment where the group members get to explore in an honest fashion who they are, how who they are impacts the
other people in the group, and finally how they fit into
the world at large.

It's in the safety of these groups that we explore how our
unfinished business seeps into our adult lives. Seeing is
believing. The group provides the context for a place to heal
the wounds that continue to fester in our day-to-day lives.

How about you? Can you think of events that

continue to reappear in your life over and over again? A certain kind of relationship? The same problems at work? Unable to break out of the trap of a compulsive behavior?

List at least three things that continually reappear in your life, something that just never goes away, something that brings you pain time and time again?

_____

_____

_____

_____

_____

_____

_____

_____

_____

_____

_____

_____

_____

Now think for a moment. What's the lesson to be learned from each of those events that continue to reappear in your life?

_____

_____

_____

_____

_____

_____

_____
_____
_____
_____
_____
_____
_____
_____
_____
_____
_____
_____
_____
_____
_____
_____
_____
_____
_____
_____
_____
_____
_____
_____

The point is that no one is immune to this simple law of life. All of us need to develop an understanding of what makes us do, say, and feel the things we do. The benefit is clear. Doing so enables us to live a *clean* life where we better understand our place in the world and the choices we've made in order to claim that spot.

259

Pathfinder's Compass

Stepping out of the shadows is a process in which we focus on the nail we are hammering, rather than day-dreaming about the house we are going to build.

We were finishing up the first session. He asked a question that most clients of mine wonder about.

"How long is all of this going to take?"

"I don't know. Just what is it that you want for yourself?" I asked.

"I want to be healthy. I want to be able to stay in a relationship without messing it up the way I always do. I can't keep on losing job after job. I have to find a way to not be involved so much with my family.

"You mean to tell me you can't tell me how long that is going to take?"

"Well, no. You see you've told me how you want the last page of your book to read, but you haven't told me what the chapters of the book are, you haven't told me how you intend to live the words of each chapter.

"Let me ask you, Irvin, can you tell me how long it'll take you to act in a loving way towards yourself in the moment? Can you tell me how long it'll take you to stop going to war with every driver who doesn't drive the way you would have them drive? Can you tell me how long it'll take for you to surrender your way of being in the world for a new and different way? Can you tell me how long it'll take you to heal the wounds that live within you? Can you..."

"All right, all right, I get your point, but you must be able to give me some idea."

"No, you don't get my point. What you want for yourself is a finished product, what I want for you is a way of life that you live and breathe each and every moment. That can happen for you right now."

Don't lose sight of this point. Take your eye off the outcome. The outcome will happen for you if, and only if, you stay focused on the steps of the journey.

Free yourself from the expectations of being perfect— doing it perfectly. Free yourself from the unobtainable standards that you set for yourself. Free yourself from the dualities of good and bad, right and wrong, kind and cruel.

Don't get lost in the completion of the project, because the point of our journey is to become more comfortable with *being* rather than living in the trap of always *doing*.

We need to embrace the magic of the moment. We need to measure those moments not by how well we're rewarded by them, but by how each moment offers one more kernel of Truth, one more morsel of experience, an experience that enables us to become who we genuinely are.

How best to benefit from the path we're creating for ourselves? Start with this: our growth, our transformation is built upon a foundation. Discover *who we are* rather than pursue the *ideal* that we are not.

Pathfinder's Compass

Stepping out of the shadows is a process of
reclaiming all of who we are.

"Now tell me again why it's so damn important for me to feel my feelings. What's the big deal? Why would I want to go through all of that suffering all over again?"

"You don't see the value of being whole?" I asked.

"Listen, don't start using that stuff on me. I asked about my feelings. That stuff's in my past. Why can't I just forget about it?"

"You don't see the value in taking ownership of all your life experiences, even the painful ones?"

"Not particularly. Why stir everything up again? I manage to cope. Now, you gotta give me that much. A person my age, the things I've been through, the way I've managed to glue my life back together. What more is there to all of this?"

"You don't see the value in feeling a sense of integration, that all of the pieces inside fit, that they somehow come together in a way that makes sense?"

"No, not really, I've gotten use to the noise. I've gotten used to the push-and-pull, starting-and-stopping, going off in one direction, then coming back from another direction. I've gotten used to all of the commotion on the inside, the resultant confusion on the outside."

"You don't see the value in silencing the noise, the

fear, the mistrust, the hunger for love and acceptance? You don't see the value in quenching the thirst you have for a purposeful life?"

"Yea, I guess I do but not if it's going to hurt this much."

All of this work, all of this growth through healing and expanding, all of this transformation through letting go and starting anew. Why should we? What for?

What we're really trying to do is create a wonderful mosaic. A mosaic constructed from all the various parts of who we are. A mosaic that includes all of our rough edges. All of those edges that we've believed for so long we had to either smooth or hide altogether.

But here's the means by which we set ourselves free. Set ourselves free from the energy we've invested in dis-owning the many parts of who we are. Now's the time to create a wondrous tapestry out of all of who we are, as well as all that we've experienced.

No longer do we need to rely on baling wire to hold ourselves together. Walking through life feeling frag-mented, have we really understood the inherent paradox of healing? Healing occurs by walking through the painful act of reclaiming all of the bits and pieces of who we are.

The act of stepping out of the shadows, the act of reclaiming begins by extending ourselves permission. Permission to *just be*. Let that roll over you for a couple of minutes. How does that sit with you?

Permission to surrender the vigilance we maintain over ourselves. Do you understand how many of us live our lives in a panic? A panic fanned by the inherent fear of *just being*. Being careful not to let anything leak out.

We have so carefully compartmentalized ourselves. Now, I'm suggesting that we stop doing that—that we take the brakes off. Oh, don't worry, even if you're open to my suggestion, it won't happen all at once.

But picture it for a moment. All the edges, all of them out in the open, maybe even in a playful way. Discovering other people who've given their edges permission to come out and play.

What I'm suggesting is that fun should be waiting for anyone who's decided to step out of the shadows. Oh sure, it's scary. It has its moments of loneliness, even regrets. But the simple act of permission can give birth to an avalanche.

An avalanche of joy. A time in your life when you no longer have to be on guard. You no longer have to be so controlled in what you do. No longer having to hold your breath every moment, always vigilant to how others are reacting to you. All the guesswork in trying to figure out what others want you to be.

No, freedom affords its own way of life—a lightness towards yourself, a carefree, playful attitude with others.

These are the rewards that await you. And it's true what I said earlier. We deserve to bring all of who we are to the table. We're deserving of a life where discouragement is a moment in time, not a way of life. We deserve the benefits from a life of knowing our place in this world affords us. And the path is a simple one. We merely need to reclaim *all* of who we are.

Pathfinder's Compass

*Do not despair about the setbacks you encounter on
your path: for it is from these very errors that we can
discover the Truth about our journey.*

This one is very counter-intuitive to everything that
we believe to be true. "We have to get it right," "We have
to do it better," "We have to work harder so that we can
be the best." Yet, I'm suggesting that you give up the
myth that your journey is about *being better at it.*

More than that, I am suggesting that wisdom is born
out of the lessons that our setbacks teach us. Embrace our
stumblings as necessary encounters with our life lessons.
Celebrate the fact that we chose to get into the game
rather than safely sit on the sidelines. There're no gifts to
be had from not trying. There's no growth to be experienced from playing it safe.

Stumbles are the only guarantees I have for you if you
choose to inch your way out of the shadows. Don't get
me wrong, I trust that a better way of life awaits you, as
well. But the only sure thing is that when we're moving
around in the dark, we're all going to trip over ourselves.

Expect it. Celebrate it. Embrace the stumbles, each
and every one of them. Discouragement is inevitable.
Let's acknowledge that from the outset. But any life experience that doesn't test you, will never bear the fruit
you're hoping for.

You can see it quite clearly, I hope. The rhythm of

life's nothing more than the ebb and flow we experience from the series of tests that the universe serves us. Avoid, at all costs, an overabundance of caution. Sure, it leaves you unprotected. But come on now, raise your hand if this is true for you, hasn't self-protection grown into insulation? Haven't we crossed the line between the appropriate need to protect ourselves and completely insulating ourselves from who we are as well as the people in our lives?

That's where we all have the most opportunity for movement. Unwrapping ourselves. Discovering new pieces of ourselves that can support us as we try new experiences, and inevitably, fall down and pick ourselves back up again. These are the pieces of ourselves that'll lead us to a life of fun and experimentation. *Embrace those pieces* and give them permission to come out and play.

Let me end this section by sharing with you the words of Ralph Waldo Emerson who I think has captured the essence of the *Rhythm of Life*, "Do not be too timid and squeamish about your actions. All life is an experiment."

Ending on a High Note

Be patient toward all that is unsolved in your heart
and try to love the questions themselves
like locked rooms and like books
that are written in a very foreign tongue.

-Ranier Maria Rilke

Some people go to book stores to find an old folk tale. I go to furniture stores. You see, when I first moved to Chicago, I discovered an old furniture store on Clark Street. I needed furniture and this place looked interesting. There were display windows in front of the building that looked like Lincoln was in office the last time they were cleaned.

Inside, I met Al, the store's owner. Al wore a cap that was much like a sea captain's hat. He walked around the store entertaining everyone that walked in.

I loved his stories, so I would visit Al's store as often as I could. Every piece of old furniture I pointed to, Al had a story to tell me. If I pointed to a table, Al would say, "That table was once owned by Marcel Saint duPont, one of Chicago's most noted shoemakers."

If I pointed to a chair, he would say, "Mary Astor loved that piece. You know, I think they named Astor Street for her."

One afternoon I saw an old wooden chair up against the far back wall of the store. The arm had fallen off and the back had spindles that shook when the chair stood still, but I loved it. I asked Al if I could buy that chair.

"Steve, that chair was once owned by one of the most interesting dancers in the history of our city. It was commissioned in Europe for a birthday celebration. Every evening following her performance, she'd sit and relax in this chair. It was known for its unique ability to fit the contours of the human body, even though it was made of wood, not fabric."

"So how much?" I asked.

"It's hard to put a price on such a valuable piece," Al

said, "but for you, I'll charge one dollar."

"One dollar?" I exclaimed.

"Yes, only a dollar. And the promise that you treat it with respect."

"How can you sell such a treasure so cheaply?" I asked.

"The chair will not be so cheap," he corrected. "You will end up paying more for it than you would for a new piece of furniture. Because in order to use the chair correctly, you must enlist the help of someone who can show you how to put it back together properly. Take it to a woodworker and ask them to show you where to find the tools and material so that you may restore the chair.

"Then you must find someone willing to show you how proper chairs function. A designer of good chairs is who you need for that. Then you must take your time and do the job right. You can work here on the fourth floor if you like. There's lots of extra space up there."

"Couldn't I just take it to a repairman?" I asked.

"No, then you'll not receive anything except a chair. It's better that you learn for yourself instead of having someone go through the motions for you."

I'm happy to tell you that the chair turned out beautifully, but I would never have been able to imagine just how much work was involved in owning that chair.

But I have Al to thank not only for the chair, but what that chair taught me about myself. Really, what Al taught me that day is no different than the lesson I hope you're taking from this book. I know the message he left with me has been a point of inspiration for me throughout the years. "Steve," he said, "it's not so important how well-off something is when you begin to work on it, it only matters how well-off it is when you finish with it."

If you've stayed with me throughout this book, I hope that you've begun to discover that same lesson for yourself. There's nothing simple about the act of stepping out of the shadows. But there's a simple formula to follow to create the kind of life that we all are longing for.

Don't be waiting for moments of profound clarity about what to do next. I hope you've embraced the idea that the next small, simple act is the most empowering act in our arsenal. Stepping out of the shadows is like unraveling a knot. You have to keep tugging at the knot, you won't unravel it with just one yank.

Think integration. Think being whole. Think about reclaiming. That's what all of this work's geared towards. North meeting south. East meeting west. The thread that we use to weave this tapestry is the song in our soul. The song that sings our life's story. The words of the song belts out the Truth about ourselves and our destiny.

The needle that pulls the thread is our spirit. Our spirit is this incredible well of energy. Sadly, this energy oftentimes lies dormant within ourselves. But, that can so easily change. We can liberate the energy of our spirit. And it can be done with one subtle shift in how we live our lives.

All we need do to harvest the wealth that awaits us by awakening our soul and liberating our spirit is follow one simple law. I call it the *Law of What's Possible*. All we need do is open ourselves to what's possible. When we're open to the possibilities of what the universe has to offer us, then we'll be open to discovering what our lives can be.

But, don't forget the importance of our mindset. We have to see the world through a different set of lenses. Unless we transform how we think about the things in our lives, it'll be difficult to see what possibilities exist in our lives.

Let me toss in one last element in this formula. Healing. Healing from within. Healing how we think about ourselves, act towards ourselves, and feel towards ourselves. Healing the way we relate to the world, the people in our lives. The salve to those tender wounds won't go on easily. It won't feel natural to the touch, but give it time, let it soak in. Let this magical salve turn old scar tissue into new tender skin. The salve I'm talking about is two magical words, *I deserve.*

That's the thought I want to leave you with. This book is nothing more than a testimony to what can happen for you when you begin to live those two words. Don't be put off by such simplicity. You needn't search for more complex solutions, although I assure you they exist.

As I say good-bye to you, do me one last honor. Look at where you are. Look to where the light is shining brightest. Take one small step towards that light, step away from the darkness of the shadows, begin your journey, and know that you deserve to be wherever that journey takes you.

G.B.U.

Steve

Notes

Notes

OTHER BOOKS AVAILABLE BY
DR. STEVE FRISCH, PSY.D.

Building Better Bridges:
Creating Great Relationships With the
People Who Matter Most

Moving Mountains:
Magical Choices For Empowering Your Life's Journey

Stepping Out of the Shadows
[Re]Connecting With Your Life's Journey

Making Molehills Out of Mountains:
Reclaiming Your Personal Power in Your Relationships

Stopping the Cycle of Self-Sabotage:
Making Your Relationships Safe and Fulfilling

To order Call (773) 477-8959 or write to:
Alive And Well Publications,
826 W. Armitage Chicago, IL 60614

Visit our website to order Dr. Frisch's, Psy.D.
books as well as other books that focus on the
mind, body, and soul at:
www.aliveandwellnews.com

HOW TO CONTACT
DR. FRISCH, PSY.D.

Dr. Frisch, Psy.D. is a clinical psychologist in private practice in Chicago, Illinois. He consults with both individuals and organizations seeking to maximize their inter personal and professional potential.

All of Dr. Frisch's,Psy.D. programs are designed to enhance each participant's emotional and spiritual well-being. Each program participant is guided on a journey that will enable them to develop the skills necessary to create a meaningful life that expresses who that person genuinely is. This is done by developing the tools necessary to enhance the relationships one has with themselves and the people in their life.

Requests for information about these services, as well as inquiries about Dr. Frisch's, Psy.D.availability for speeches, workshops, and seminars, should be directed to Dr. Frisch, Psy.D. at the address below.

You can contact Dr. Frisch, Psy.D. at
Alive And Well Publications
826 W. Armitage
Chicago, Illinois, 60614
(773) 477-8959.

You can also contact Dr. Frisch, Psy.D. through
Alive And Well Publications' website at:
www.aliveandwellnews.com

The Secret To Personal Empowerment?

Are you ready to transform your life today? *Moving Mountains–Magical Choices for Empowering Your Life's Journey*, provides a deceivingly simple yet powerful formula for transcending your fears in order to create a life of emotional and spiritual well-being.

Dr. Frisch, Psy.D. details remarkably powerful steps from which you can create your own blueprint for emotional and spiritual well-being. For example, Dr. Frisch writes, "To transform your life, you only need to create different choices by combining new ways of thinking and acting." The means to do so? You will learn how to:

- **Unleash the Forces of Personal Empowerment**
- **Expand Your Personal Choices**
- **Widen Your World View**
- **Master the Five Tools of Actions**

If you want to think of yourself differently, see yourself differently, carry yourself differently, and ultimately be treated differently by others, *Moving Mountains* is the perfect vehicle to get you there.

To order by phone, call (312) 787-3412
To order by mail, send a check or money order for $12.95 plus $5.00 S&H. Illinois residents include sales tax of $1.13 per book ordered. Alive And Well Publications, 826 West Armitage, Chicago, Illinois, 60614

Moving Mountains

Dr. Steve Frisch, Psy. D.
Magical Choices For Empowering Your Life's Journey

The Secret To Transforming Your Life?

How do you create a life that reflects the essence of who you are? How do you reconnect with those parts of yourself you disowned so long ago? How do you create a life that honors your voice from within? *Stepping Out of The Shadows: [Re]Connecting with Your Life's Journey* is the perfect guide for anybody searching for the means to create a deeper sense of purpose in their lives as well as a deeper connection to the underlying forces of life.

Dr. Frisch, Psy.D. describes the process we all experience as we pursue our natural urge to grow and evolve. *Stepping Out of The Shadows* demystifies the process of enriching your emotional and spiritual well-being. You will discover how to create a personal blueprint that will enable you to:

- **Awaken Your Soul**
- **Liberate Your Spirit**
- **Illuminate Your Path**
- **Transform Your Mindset**

If you want to activate the process of healing and life transformation, *Stepping Out of The Shadows* is the perfect catalyst to begin your journey.

To order by phone, call (312) 787-3412

To order by mail, send a check or money order for $18.95 plus $5.00 S&H. Illinois residents include sales tax of $1.65 per book ordered. Alive And Well Publications, 826 West Armitage, Chicago, Illinois, 60614

The Secret of How To Love and Be Loved?

Loving relationships are created by using simple to use relationship skills that enable two people to navigate the inevitable choppy waters in any relationship. The most important relationship skill of them all? Dr. Steve Frisch, Psy.D. says that mastering the art of resolving unacknowledged, unresolved relationship issues is the single most important relationship skill of them all.

Making Molehills Out of Mountains: Reclaiming Your Personal Power in Your Relationships discusses a unique process of conflict resolution that will enable you to discover the joy of reclaiming your personal power in all of your relationships. By combining very simple to use relationship skills with a heightened self-awareness, you'll create open, caring, relationships with the people who matter most.

You'll learn how to:

- **Become as expert at resolving conflict as you are at creating it.**
- **Stop sabotaging your relationships by learning how to end your never ending patterns of conflict.**
- **Successfully resolve relationship issues rather than continually fail at fixing relationship problems.**

If you're searching for a deeper understanding of yourself and the conflicts you create in your relationships, *Making Molehills Out of Mountains* is the book for you.

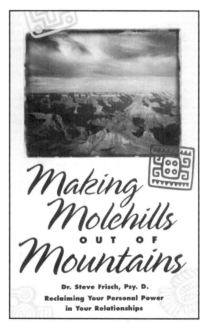

To order by phone, call (312) 787-3412
To order by mail, send a check or money order for $18.95 plus $5.00 S&H. Illinois residents include sales tax of $1.65 per book ordered. Alive And Well Publications, 826 West Armitage, Chicago, Illinois, 60614

Come Visit Us on the Internet!

http://www.aliveandwellnews.com

Come see what we have for you at our web site!

- **Free newsletters** filled with information that will enrich your mind, body, and soul!

- **Free special reports** filled with information to enhance your emotional, physical, and spiritual well-being!

- **Free chapters** from Dr. Frisch's, Psy.D. collection of books and workbooks that focus on relationship bridge-building and life transformation!

- **Special offers** on our complete selection of personal growth audio tapes!

- **Special offers** on Dr Frisch's, Psy.D. books available through our web site!

- **Gift certificates** to purchase products and services from many of our contributing authors!